TWO SCHOOLS OF COOL

TWO SCHOOLS OF COOL

- Sarah Cain and George Herms
- Stanya Kahn and Llyn Foulkes
- Shana Lutker and John Baldessari
- Amanda Ross-Ho and Allen Ruppersberg
- Robert Williams and Ed Moses

Curated by Sarah C. Bancroft

Orange County Museum of Art
Newport Beach, California

Fellows of Contemporary Art
Los Angeles

DelMonico Books • Prestel
Munich London New York

This catalog was published in conjunction with the exhibition *Two Schools of Cool*, curated by Sarah C. Bancroft and organized and presented by the Orange County Museum of Art, Newport Beach, California, October 9, 2011–January 22, 2012.

Two Schools of Cool was initiated and is sponsored by the Fellows of Contemporary Art. Additional support is provided by the Beall Family Foundation.

Published by
Orange County Museum of Art
850 San Clemente Drive
Newport Beach, CA 92660
USA
Tel +1 949-759-1122
Fax +1 949-759-5623
www.ocma.net

Fellows of Contemporary Art
970 N. Broadway, Suite 208
Los Angeles, CA 90012
USA
Tel +1 213-808-1008
Fax +1 213-808-1018
www.focala.org

Distributed by DelMonico Books,
an imprint of Prestel
Prestel is a member of Verlagsgruppe
Random House GmbH

Prestel Verlag
Neumarkter Strasse 28
81673 Munich
Germany
Tel 49 89 242908 300
Fax 49 89 242908 335
prestel.de

Prestel Publishing Ltd.
4 Bloomsbury Place
London WC1A 2QA
United Kingdom
Tel 44 20 7323 5004
Fax 44 20 7636 8004

Prestel Publishing
900 Broadway, Suite 603
New York, NY 10003
Tel 212 995 2720
Fax 212 995 2733
sales@prestel-usa.com
prestel.com

ISBN: 978-3-7913-5188-9

Editor: Karen Jacobson
Designer: Michael Worthington, Counterspace, Los Angeles
Principal photographer: Joshua White
Proofreader: Dianne Woo
Color separation: Echelon Color, Venice, California
Printer: The Avery Group, Shapco Printing, Minneapolis

Contents

Foreword

When the Newport Harbor Art Museum, a predecessor of the Orange County Museum of Art, opened in 1962, it was one of the few venues for contemporary art in Southern California. During its first two decades, the museum organized exhibitions that presented groundbreaking works by most of the established artists in *Two Schools of Cool*, including John Baldessari, Llyn Foulkes, George Herms, Ed Moses, and Allen Ruppersberg. In the last five years, works by all the younger participants in this project have likewise been shown at the museum.

Two Schools of Cool is an experimental exhibition pairing two different generations of artists to create collaborative works. The open, fluid structure of the project is indicative of the museum's focus on innovation in curatorial practice, new scholarship on contemporary art, and public engagement with the most compelling art and artists of our time.

Two Schools of Cool received leadership support from the Fellows of Contemporary Art, and we are supremely grateful for the Fellows' full embrace of the project from the outset. We also thank the Beall Family Foundation for its outstanding contribution to the project.

Our trustees likewise make possible so much of what we do, and their belief in and support of this exhibition exemplify our museum's commitment to excellence. Behind the scenes of any exhibition is the museum's talented staff–including the development, education, facilities, marketing, registration, and visitor services departments–and we are sincerely grateful for their dedication to our mission.

Finally, curator Sarah Bancroft is to be applauded for bravely organizing a bold, experimental project that pushes the boundaries of individual practice, as are the artists John Baldessari, Sarah Cain, Llyn Foulkes, George Herms, Stanya Kahn, Shana Lutker, Ed Moses, Amanda Ross-Ho, Allen Ruppersberg, and Robert Williams for taking this journey with us. These ten artists engaged with the idea of collaboration to develop new forms, dialogues, and expressions, rewarding us with five stellar and distinct installations that remain true to the artists' individual visions.

Dennis Szakacs
Director
Orange County Museum of Art

Sponsor's Statement

In almost forty years of funding exhibitions and artists, the Fellows of Contemporary Art (FOCA) has remained steadfast in its support of and commitment to California art and has been adept at selecting innovative and timely exhibitions. The 2011 Curator's Award exhibition, *Two Schools of Cool*, curated by Sarah Bancroft, continues the Fellows' tradition of insightful and timely support of provocative but often underrecognized curatorial premises. We are so pleased that this year's venue, the Orange County Museum of Art, embraces our belief that experimental, collaborative, and risk-taking projects are what contemporary art museums are all about. It is thrilling to know that after so many years and more than forty exhibitions, FOCA continues to be on the cutting edge, fostering curators and artists and expressing its faith in the process of artistic creation.

On behalf of FOCA, I would like to congratulate the artists, curator Sarah Bancroft, director Dennis Szakacs, and everyone else at the Orange County Museum of Art for this extraordinary exhibition and accompanying catalog. *Two Schools of Cool* offers a unique view of cross-generational artistic collaboration, a laboratory-style curatorial approach, and a printed document that miraculously captures the spirit of this daring experiment of pairing California icons with their new-millennium colleagues. It is interesting to note that FOCA's very first exhibition was devoted to *Two Schools of Cool* artist Ed Moses in 1976; our history also includes several group shows featuring the work of John Baldessari and a solo exhibition for Llyn Foulkes in 1995.

I would also like to acknowledge Mary Chabre, recent past chair of the FOCA Long Range Planning Committee, whose unwavering support for the grant-making process kept everything on track, and her successor, Bob Myers, for keeping the torch burning. And I thank Mary Leigh Cherry, the exhibition liaison, for her unflappable commitment to the project as the intermediary between the museum and FOCA, and for her contagious enthusiasm for the project.

On the occasion of the presentation of *Two Schools of Cool* and the publication of this catalog, we thank our members, past and present, for their support of contemporary art in California. We would not be here without you. And a special thank-you to you, the viewer, for making it all worthwhile.

Greg Karns
Chair, Board of Directors
Fellows of Contemporary Art

Acknowledgments

This exhibition grew out of an invitation in 2009 from the Fellows of Contemporary Art, which suggested that I apply for the 2011 Curator's Award. The Fellows selected my proposal for *Two Schools of Cool* out of the fifty or so submitted, and I thank the organization for its bravery. FOCA has a remarkable and long-standing commitment to art, artists, and curators in the state of California. The artists featured in the exhibition followed suit by agreeing to work in pairs that I had in most cases suggested and by formulating—according to their own definitions of collaboration—compelling projects. They have made this concept their own, a curatorial lab that became a creative, experimental exhibition that continues to challenge and inspire me. The artists have my everlasting gratitude.

No exhibition is brought to fruition without the help and talents of museum colleagues. Anna Brouwer, former publications manager, proved a key supporter in the early stages of this project. Fatima Manalili, curatorial associate, brought her calm attention to myriad aspects of the exhibition and catalog, including compiling the artists' biographies in this volume. The facilities and registrarial staffs—including Albert Lopez Jr., director of operations; Anna-Marie Sanchez, exhibitions and collections manager; Jeanette Saunders, registrar; and Ed Bopp, assistant registrar—have all played a role in realizing the installation of this exhibition. Kirsten Schmidt, director of marketing and communications, has done a superb job of promoting a "unique" exhibition concept. Lisa Silagyi, director of education and public programs, and her competent team—Kelly Bishop, Dorothy McClelland, and Jenni Stenson—have created education and public programs that are an important complement to the exhibition. Our development department and special events staff—including Darcy Schwier, Bridget Jesionowski-McKay, and Kate Andersen—are likewise to be thanked for their superb efforts, as are Hayley Miller, director of visitor services, and Steve Schmidt, security coordinator. I especially thank director Dennis Szakacs and our board of trustees for giving this exhibition concept a home, and for their ongoing commitment to contemporary art and experimentation. I also join Dennis in thanking the Beall Family Foundation for providing important additional support for this project, which enabled its realization.

The catalog has benefited greatly from the efforts and insights of Constance Lewallen, Phyllis Lutjeans, Andy Moses, and Catherine Taft, who have deftly worked with the artists and me on the interviews for this publication. I am also grateful for the talents of our catalog designer, Michael Worthington, who has produced a strong publication that reflects the spirit of the exhibition. Likewise, Karen Jacobson has adeptly edited the texts, going above and beyond the call of duty, for which I am most thankful. Joshua White and his able staff provided superb photography of the exhibition, and Tony Manzella at Echelon masterfully oversaw the production of color separations for the catalog. We are delighted that the book is being distributed by the capable and energetic Mary DelMonico of DelMonico Books · Prestel.

Abby and Andreas Beroutsos, Tony Shafrazi, Suzanne Williams, and a private collector who wishes to remain anonymous graciously parted with works from their collections for the benefit of the artists' installations. Many individuals at the artists' studios and galleries were likewise exceptionally helpful with information, insight, and images, including Rebecca Camacho at Anthony Meier Fine Arts; Carol Lewis at Ed Moses's studio; Hiroko Onoda, director of the Tony Shafrazi Gallery, and her colleague George Horner; and Laura Watts at Honor Fraser Gallery. I am deeply grateful to Mary Leigh Cherry, who sits on the Long Range Planning Committee of the Fellows of Contemporary Art. She served as a stalwart liaison between the museum and the Fellows, ensuring the clear communication and forward momentum that are essential to a successful collaboration.

I would also like to thank the late Dennis Hopper, who agreed early on, without hesitation, to participate as an artist in the exhibition before succumbing to a long illness. Caroline Huber graciously provided information and enthusiastic support for the project. Walter Hopps, as well, is an uncredited collaborator on this project. The exhibition is both a loving tribute to my former colleague and mentor and his rich history in Los Angeles and a reflection of the city's contemporary art world and my own independent career path. The arts scene in Los Angeles and Southern California continues to develop, strong and distinct, having grown from its vibrant beginnings at midcentury into the diverse, multigenerational community represented in this exhibition and publication. *Two Schools of Cool* is meant to explore, transcend, and celebrate these rich histories, especially the artists across generations who have come here to study, work, teach, and explore, and who have become part of the ever-growing and evolving fabric of this creative community.

Sarah C. Bancroft
Curator

Two Schools of Cool: Sarah C. Bancroft and Phyllis Lutjeans in Conversation

PL: With a show like this, the thing I find interesting is that it raises the question of whether collaboration redefines the function of the artist, the single artist. If it does, how does it do that? And does it even matter? Many major exhibitions focus on the practice and history of the artist and somehow leave the actual art lurking around somewhere. The art becomes secondary to the art historical analysis or the examination of the cultural history. But for the viewer who has a basic affinity for art and is looking for another way to approach it, the art becomes the most important thing. Over the years there has been collaboration everywhere, going back to the Renaissance, but often collaborators don't get credit. Here is a new show in which two artists collaborate as if they are one, and the viewer will view the result as one work if it's a true collaboration. You don't know what's going to happen, do you?

SB: Well, I have project descriptions from all the artists, so I have a really good idea of what they're working on. I'm very comfortable with letting their process roll out. I trust them as collaborators, and they are also collaborating with me and the institution. I'm also comfortable with the idea of failure. You have to be comfortable with that in order to have successes. Beyond the detailed diagrams, descriptions, layouts, and working plans, I don't know precisely what the projects will look like until they are installed—none of us do—but I know how the artists have been working and what their intent is. I am laying out the show in the galleries based on these ideas.

In terms of the collaboration and what happens to the artists' identities and to the artwork itself, the exhibition from the beginning was and is a laboratory. What happens when artists work together in likely and unlikely pairs, artists from an older generation who are part of the rich fabric of L.A. working with those who are more recent contributors to this vibrant community? You know, people often say that L.A. has no history. Many of the artists in the show made history; they were working here in the late 1950s and the 1960s, when L.A. became a burgeoning art community. Since then, the city has grown into an international art center. This is a specific moment in time—*now*—when you can still work alongside many of the founders, those who were here getting the ball rolling, and that won't always be the case. "Contemporary art" can be work developed by the founders and/or art by younger artists working here now.

What happens if you give people the opportunity to work together—the early explorers with the new guard? You don't see a lot of intergenerational collaboration here (except in the university setting, where you have professors working with students and whatnot). It's rare to hear older artists make unsolicited comments about the work of much younger artists. Some of the artists have never collaborated before and made a point of telling me, "I don't collaborate." And yet they found a way to approach each other, and some who were the most adamant that they weren't natural collaborators very quickly found that they were enjoying the process and were collaborating in spite of themselves. It's about opening up a possibility or many possibilities. Of course, John Baldessari does have a strong history of collaborating, and other artists in the show have collaborated as well. The collaborations speak to a continuity of the art world and its history, that it's not vacuum-packed and put on a shelf or in a book.

PL: This exhibition is seemingly outside the conventional art system, though not so much outside the art world. But an exhibition like this probably has no value in terms of selling artworks, which is often important to dealers and artists. I know you said it's a lab, but because it is "art," and because we have that innate monetary structure within the art system, it brings up other issues, which is fascinating to me. I don't know whether that crossed your mind at all in connection with the exhibition.

SB: The exhibition raises some really provoking questions. As a museum curator, I'm not selling the works as a gallery would; I'm not concerned about commercial marketability. However, I expect that once they leave the museum, some of these works will be sold by the artists' galleries, because the work is strong. (I think you're asking how commercially viable are "coauthored" works?) Some other questions: what is this object or experience or installation that's been created by two artists, how does one quantify it, and who owns it afterward? You know, the artists are coalescing an experience in space and time, an installation for people to come and see and experience, and it represents each individual artist or the collaborative pair or both. It depends. Different artists are handling this differently. Mostly it's a combined effort for each pair, truly a collaboration that each artist contributed to. They are making something for the installation, something physical or experiential or time based.

PL: That combines the ideas of both artists in a balanced way?

SB: I can't speak for the artists, but to me it seems so, yes. In all but one instance, they're creating new work together. (Ed Moses and Robert Williams are curating each other's works.) They're finding common ground between their practices and moving forward with a coherent project that works for both. And that is taking many forms. For instance, Llyn Foulkes and Stanya Kahn are working on a video together. Originally he'd agreed to write the music, and she would do the video. He showed up at her studio for the first working session with some unusual props and became more and more involved, so it's not just him making music and her making the video. They really are creating a unified project, a video in which both perform.

PL: And other artists are doing something similar?

SB: John and Shana are creating an installation that is about selection and choice on the part of the visitor. You enter a small space, where you come upon two tables with objects. You are invited to move the objects from one table to another, and people can see what you're doing via a live video feed that's projected on the outside wall. I think people who are familiar with John's career will see similarities with other works he's done and likewise that it has a lot in common with Shana's practice. They discussed and developed this project over time, with great attention. And her practice is quite distinct, but it's still a conceptual practice. Both of them address selection, choice, and interactivity in their work; she deals a lot more with memory and personal history. To me, this project potently summarizes and performs the art system that we operate in. We all make private choices—as artists, curators, or collectors—that are then played out publicly, put on display. Al and Amanda are developing a sculptural and multimedia installation that espouses both of their practices but not in the format that some may expect. (They both work with Peg-Board, but you won't see any of that in the installation.) A strong, "simple gesture" that speaks to their mutual use of archives, images, and objects. Sarah and George are choreographing an installation that corroborates their individual practices; it's a symphony composed of objects, paintings, collages, text, assemblage.

PL: What do you want the viewer to get out of this concept?

SB: Well, I can't control how the viewer approaches the work or thinks about it. A lot of people may come upon the work, and unless they read the labels, they won't necessarily realize that these are collaborative works. So they'll just approach them as objects, installations, a video, paintings, or assemblages in a room, and hopefully these artworks will draw them in, and that will lead to learning more about the show's premise. But I can't control the viewer's experience. Some ideas, interpretations, and responses that have nothing to do with my intention or the artists' are equally valid.

PL: It sounds like the unexpectedness that you anticipate in all the work is the same unexpectedness that you hope the viewer might experience.

SB: I haven't thought about it that way directly, but there's definitely truth in your statement. We know what the ideas are, we know how they're being fabricated, how physically they are being realized in the space, but what will happen in the space? How will people interact with them? People are left in the space with the art, not the artist. The artist kind of goes away, and the curator goes away, so there's an element of surprise because whether you know something about the artist or not, at the end of the day you're left with an installation and a wall label. You can see their fingerprints in it, but it's more about the work and less about the artists' unique identities.

PL: That's how I think it should be too. But you did select artists who are well known.

SB: Yes, absolutely.

PL: That makes it interesting, just in and of itself.

SB: Well, it makes people curious.

PL: And you selected the artist pairs to collaborate. Did you at one time consider letting the artists pick their partners?

SB: No, I was interested in curating the pairs and letting the artists develop their projects. Rather than cherry-pick the artwork, which is what curators usually do, I was picking the artist pairs. But I knew that there would inevitably be changes from my original suggestions, fissures in my concept.

There are artists who are very clearly natural pairs. And others who are a little unexpected, more challenging. And that was part of the experience too. What happens when you ask people to work on something? It wasn't their idea to work together, but they could develop whatever they wanted as a collaborative project. Will they go there, will they do that, is the exhibition idea even interesting? Does it have legs? I had to go through this whole process to find out. I'm very grateful that the artists, for the most part, were incredibly open to the idea.

I had originally thought to put Stanya and another artist (who is in the show) together, and it didn't work out, and that was part of the process. Ultimately she suggested working with the stellar Llyn Foulkes, and it was a brilliant choice. They have developed a strong, fascinating collaboration. In most cases, my pairings stuck, but in that instance it went in another direction, and that's a positive development.

PL: When you approached the artists, how did they respond to your idea of selecting the artists?

SB: Not all of them knew each other, so some people asked for more information on the artist I was suggesting. I didn't feel odd suggesting the pairs. Amanda Ross-Ho and Allen Ruppersberg didn't know each other personally; he had recently seen her work at MoMA in a photography show, and she was well aware of his practice. When we met at Amanda's studio, they immediately hit it off. Conceptually they found a lot of common ground, and we all knew that pairing was going to fly. They quickly discovered mutual affinities. John and Shana both immediately agreed, and John told me then that Shana had been a student of his at UCLA. (I wasn't aware of that when I paired them.) George Herms and Sarah Cain knew each other and were happy to work together (George notably calls it "corroboration" rather than collaboration). Ed and Robert are great fans of each other's work but are from very different sectors of the art universe. If Ed is the proton, Bob is the electron circulating around a nucleus, equally important but serving as an ionizing force in some way. If you're asking me why I paired certain people, sometimes it was conceptual or about process, an intriguing similarity or polarity.

PL: So here you have older artists and younger artists in the context of Los Angeles art history. How would a show like this be documented? Would it fall into an art historical category?

SB: It certainly addresses the history of Los Angeles, but it doesn't fall into an easy category in terms of chronology. You can have older and younger artists working alongside each other, collaborating, in a nonhierarchical way. People look at artists and their careers, art history and the canon, in a teleological fashion, looking backward, who begat whom, as if it's all a progression. But that's not really true. Influences flow in many directions. So I really don't know where this show will fall in art history; it's not for me to decide. You know, it was a unique opportunity for me to work with artists with very different practices, very different histories that feed each other and are actually interrelated. And for the artists to do so. And personally I can engage with artists of my own generation as well as artists who are august Los Angeles figures. And part of my interest in this exhibition had to do with Walter Hopps, whom I worked with earlier in my career.

Walter spent a lot of time talking about his early years in L.A. And here I was, a young curator working in New York, cocurating a James Rosenquist retrospective with Walter at the Guggenheim. I was working with the establishment at the start. So my career felt kind of backwards.

PL: To start working with the older artists instead of the younger ones?

SB: Yes, I was working with artists who had already had long, successful careers, but what about also working with artists from my own generation? That really interested me after a while. (I was extremely curious about and envious of those working with up-and-coming artists and projects.)

PL: It's one thing to say that this show is a lab—let's just see what comes out of it—but there's some other modus operandi here, whether you know that now or not.

SB: There's more than one locus. I think the show will continue to change after it opens and, more importantly, after it closes. That's true of any show. It has a life beyond the curator. If you were to ask me what the purpose is, what was the seed of the show, there are many answers to that question. How did the show come about? Part of it is me wanting to continue working with the elder statesmen and -women, so to speak, but also to work with my own generation.

PL: I think that's an important clue, absolutely.

SB: And it's addressing my own history with Walter and in Los Angeles. The show makes an important point that artists can function in a nonhierarchical way, not based on age or historical cliques. This goes back to George Herms, whom we both know well. George was a really important catalyst for this exhibition. We were talking over a meal, and he mentioned a young artist whom he really liked. He wasn't talking about her by name; he was describing her works on paper as exquisite corpses and how there were certain affinities in their practices that involved text and collage. When I asked who the artist was, he said it was Sarah Cain. They had become friends at Skowhegan. And I know Sarah's work; I love her work, and I thought, *Wow, this is a rare moment.* This is awkward to say, but it's a rare occurrence when an older established artist talks about a much younger artist in a complimentary way.

PL: Yes.

SB: As a curator, I've rarely experienced it, and I thought, *Okay, George is George; he's not your average dude.* [*Laughter.*] He doesn't operate as most people do, and it was just a powerful moment. And I wondered what would happen if I put other artists together, younger and older—would they be able to achieve the same cohesion? Would the older artists be open to it? I thought beforehand, in my own bias, that the younger artists would be enthusiastic and the older artists might be more hesitant. And in the end, most everyone that I asked participated.

PL: This is really important to understanding the foundation of the show, the concept, your own personal searching. I think the show is answering questions for you personally.

SB: Maybe. I haven't thought about that.

PL: Because everybody says about you, "Oh my god, she's so young and she's working with this artist and that artist, all these famous artists, blah, blah, blah." That must have influenced your thinking.

SB: Not really. [*Laughter.*] And I'm not that young. [*Laughter.*]

PL: That's what you're saying. But you don't know. Because of what's happened with your career, I think there is some kind of a searching that's connected with this show. I can't explain it, but it's very personal.

SB: That's a very interesting way of approaching it. I hadn't thought about that.

PL: It's very personal, maybe more personal than you were anticipating.

SB: I always knew there was a personal element, but the public element, the questions I'm asking the artists and the art world are quite significant. And then the backstory is how my history influences the concept for the show.

PL: Yeah, the conception of it really comes from that.

SB: It does. Well, and the other element I don't discuss much, and I like leaving it open, is that most of the pairs are made up of an older artist who is male and a younger artist who is female. If you watch the film *The Cool School*, documenting the Ferus Gallery in the 1960s, it was all about the "studs"—all guys. There was a lot of testosterone in that film. As a woman (who considers herself a feminist), I wanted the show to acknowledge the shifts that have happened in the art world. The opportunities have expanded; the purview has expanded to include many more people.

PL: I think you should bring this up, without making it into a political statement. At one time, this would never have happened.

SB: Well, it should be unnoteworthy, unsensational that there are female artists collaborating with male artists. This is why I don't note it, for the most part. And it's more interesting–to me–to see who notices. And who doesn't. Who is focused on the work and why the pairings are good pairings in their own right (based on the artists' practices) or compelling or challenging, without making the fact that there are all these women with all these older men a main focus. Because the exhibition can operate without a hierarchy based on age, an implied patriarchy or chauvinism, just as the artwork does; the artwork just is.

PL: But the critics are going to say, "What?"

SB: Maybe.

PL: Do you want to define it?

SB: I'm not going to hit anyone over the head with it. Again, I'm asking another question, and those are the answers that will come out once the show is open. Will people focus on that, that there are pairings between men and women, or will they focus on the work, the collaborations between the artists, who are also men and women of different ages? There are kick-ass women working in L.A. today, and we should be able to take it for granted. And I do, I do take it for granted. I don't notice, oh, there are this many women artists working here and that many men, because there is no longer a distinction. They're all artists. I think it would be more notable to pair the men with younger men, in a way. Some people would notice, many would not, and those who did would have strong responses for a completely different reason.

PL: It's really important that you've talked about that personal part of it, the show, because it gives it another dimension that is not usual. Curators don't like to do that; they like to keep everything over here, you know, "objective."

SB: No exhibition is objective or totally impersonal. A curator's process is not unlike the artist's, and I'm very comfortable with that process, with this show especially. It's very different than my Diebenkorn show, however. With a monographic show like *Richard Diebenkorn: The Ocean Park Series*, if you're doing your job right, no one is thinking about you; it's seamless. People are thinking only about the artwork and whatever thesis you're trying to present in the galleries through the artwork. An exhibition like this is similar, and yet my process is very much part of the show; it's more ingrained. And I'm not ashamed to talk about that, because that's where I'm coming from. I'll probably get attacked for that.

PL: And you have to remember, too, that curators have influence. Look at Walter–he had a tremendous influence. And you know Walter has been spoken about a lot but not always in 100 percent positive terms.

SB: Well, he was human; he was very human, with an extraordinary ability, impact, and history. What I found intriguing and shocking when I moved out west was, you know, the cult of Walter, the cult surrounding him. It freaked me out. Walter was a man, and he has such a profound reputation. I worked with him; we had a very close professional relationship, and we were close friends.

PL: A bond, it sounds like a real bond.

SB: Yes. Also, I worked with him in his later years, and he'd probably mellowed out a bit. Someone said to me, "You haven't worked with Walter until he's made you cry." [*Laughter.*] But he never made me cry. He trusted me, and that was the greatest gift.

PL: Well, he must have respected you tremendously. He recognized that.

SB: He was very generous.

PL: You call it generous, but he also knew who you were, and he trusted you, and he knew your intelligence.

SB: Yeah, well, I worked my ass off. Also, I wasn't scared. Some people are like bears: they can smell fear, and they'll just tear you apart if they sense it. (But I'm not calling Walter a bear.) [*Laughter.*] Walter and Jim Rosenquist respected me and gave me the room to make decisions and really do my job. And I was like, I don't care who you are. I'm here to do a job, and we all want this to be successful. And that stood me in good stead.

I'm very quiet about my relationship with Walter. I don't bandy it around. Other than in relation to this show, I don't bring it up. I'm very possessive of it because I don't want people to consume it.

PL: How will you bring him up in connection with an exhibition like this?

SB: Well, I mention him, but it's important to note also that the Ferus Gallery was one of many exciting developments in town. Walter and Ed Kienholz and then Irving Blum were extremely important to the development of the L.A. art world, one of many fulcrums at that time. And that's why the artists in this show, the older guys, not all of them showed at Ferus. Baldessari was adamantly outside of that group, for instance. Robert Williams was in a completely different artistic universe (though he and Walter later became friends). I'm trying to show a wider arc.

Los Angeles was a creative hotbed; it was *really* happening in the 1960s. Maybe because there was "no history" and people could do whatever the hell they wanted. And so *Two Schools of Cool* is a misnomer, intentionally, because there were already more than two schools of cool back in the day, and there are more than two now. This is a very small group of artists that could never represent all the creative activity then and now. You can't simply focus on Ferus or the older artists, because L.A. was so much richer and more diverse. It's not just the artists people traditionally associate with Southern California and the Ferus scene.

There's someone like Robert Williams. He's the odd duck in the group. Some people ask me, "Why is he in there?" Well, if you're really looking at the history of L.A., you have a huge underground movement—that's no longer underground—that's related to comics, graphic novels, "lowbrow" art, custom car culture…

So I'm trying to tell it more broadly. Yes, Robert doesn't fit into what people might term the original Cool School, and yet he's a counterculture icon. He was studying at Chouinard when the Ferus guys were working here in the 1960s, and he was watching them and thinking, *My work is not going to fly in this world, I don't do abstract work, I don't do light and space or conceptual work or pop, I'm a draftsman at heart, I like cartoons.* (But the man can *paint.*) He's an interesting counterpoint in this show.

PL: Who is he working with?

SB: He's working with Ed Moses.

PL: Oh, he is, so that's the opposite direction. It will be really interesting to see how that one will come out.

SB: And they really like each other's work. For their installation, they're selecting each other's work, working on labels for each other, and we will have a public program where they critique each other's work. In every show you have to do something unexpected, push people's expectations or boundaries. Ed is part of the establishment, and Robert is the unexpected element that actually totally belongs. I feel like I'm showing a more inclusive swath of the art scene.

PL: I think the intuitive part of explaining that history and how you view it as an observer really are important; no one has done that very much. It's interesting for me to hear.

SB: I really started digging in and asking you and others about Los Angeles in the 1960s when I was researching and writing about Diebenkorn. Just how gripping and explosive that moment was in L.A. Because of the Pacific Standard Time initiative, the "tyranny of history" will play out across Southern California this fall, and it will be rewritten. A lot of people will be written in, finally. (I use *tyranny* in the sense that a lot of older work will be coming out of storage and much less work from the recent past will be on view; there won't be a lot of contemporary art on view. But the history itself is being revised, which is stupendous.)

I'm extremely happy that the show is coinciding with PST. Many of the older artists in this show are going to have historical work on view in several PST shows, and you know, they're still working! *Two Schools of Cool* is one of the few shows that will have contemporary work by younger artists on view as well.

PL: This particular show is truly a lab. And because it's a lab, it's almost outside the rim of "the art world." It's an intriguing idea to me because one doesn't know what's going to happen: you're leaving them free. It's about ideas, really.

SB: Well, I will say that there's one constraint in this show, one area where I could not give the artists absolute free rein. And that was…

PL: Obscenity, probably? [*Laughter.*]

SB: No, I don't care about that! (I'll put a sign up that says, "May not be suitable for children," and let the parents negotiate it.) It's resources. You know, I wish I could give them all the money in the world.

PL: Oh, right, yeah. There was some money, though?

SB: Yes, there is a budget for creating new work. They've worked within the budget to develop wonderful and distinct projects.

PL: That's something you should bring up, in a very subtle way, so that people get the idea that there was constraint.

SB: Yes, opportunity and constraint. I'm very grateful to the artists.

The other impetus—there's more than one germinating seed that created this exhibition—is that the Fellows of Contemporary Art asked me to apply for its 2011 Curator's Award, and I was trying to figure out what I could propose. Then I had the conversation with George about Sarah, and this is what I developed. The Fellows have a shared history with Walter and L.A. (it was originally a support group at the Pasadena Art Museum, where Walter was director) and with so many of the artists in this exhibition. There is a great deal of overlap in my interest and their history. Their invitation was significant. It was the opportunity through which the show was first germinated, and it ultimately made the realization of the project possible.

PL: I think one of the affinities you have for all this California art is through Walter.

SB: I really like the artwork. Some of the artists I knew personally through Walter; many I didn't. Some of the younger artists I knew as well, but some I didn't, and they were probably pretty surprised to hear from me. For me, the show is an act of faith.

PL: I love that idea that even more than an experiment, this is a lab. I think it fits tighter somehow.

SB: An experiment implies that this could go horribly wrong. A lab suggests that we're going to work on something here, we're going to do something here. Let's see what happens.

TWO SCHOOLS OF COOL

SARAH CAIN AND GEORGE HERMS *KORRAL*, 2011

Sarah Cain and George Herms have assembled an installation that forms a bridge between their practices as well as between language and abstraction. Cain's large- and small-scale paintings dance along two walls. Her work spills from the two-dimensional field of a painted canvas onto the floor and wall in *Untitled (Fall 2011)*, as well as in a painted silver-leafed line that completely encircles the project, floor to ceiling. Herms's found-object sculptures and assemblages congregate in two display cases and on his *Lemon Bar* table on the floor, interlope on the wall with two hanging works, and finally hang from the ceiling with five BBQ MoonRock sculptures. Theirs is an abstract composition achieved with individual works by each artist. Cain explains: "I've always gravitated toward abstraction for the openness that it allows. I use it in a way similar to the space between a hypothesis and a conclusion; it is an experimental free zone." Using an additive process, Herms and Cain have created a free zone of mutual expression that brings their work into close dialogue while successfully achieving a unified presentation. Sharing an interest in language and a frustration over its limits in describing abstract work, the artists have likewise incorporated the poem "Me and Mrs. Jones" by Duncan McNaughton and an excerpt from a letter by artist, curator, and art historian Bill Seitz that has informed their own discussions since they met at Skowhegan in 2006. Herms is a Beat generation artist-poet-performer known for found-object sculptures that established him as a founder of the California assemblage movement in the early 1960s. Cain's paintings and installations have spoken to the relevance and significance of abstraction in the new millennium, and to her nuanced sensibility as a colorist and young experienced artist.

Sarah Cain and George Herms
Korral, 2011 (installation view)

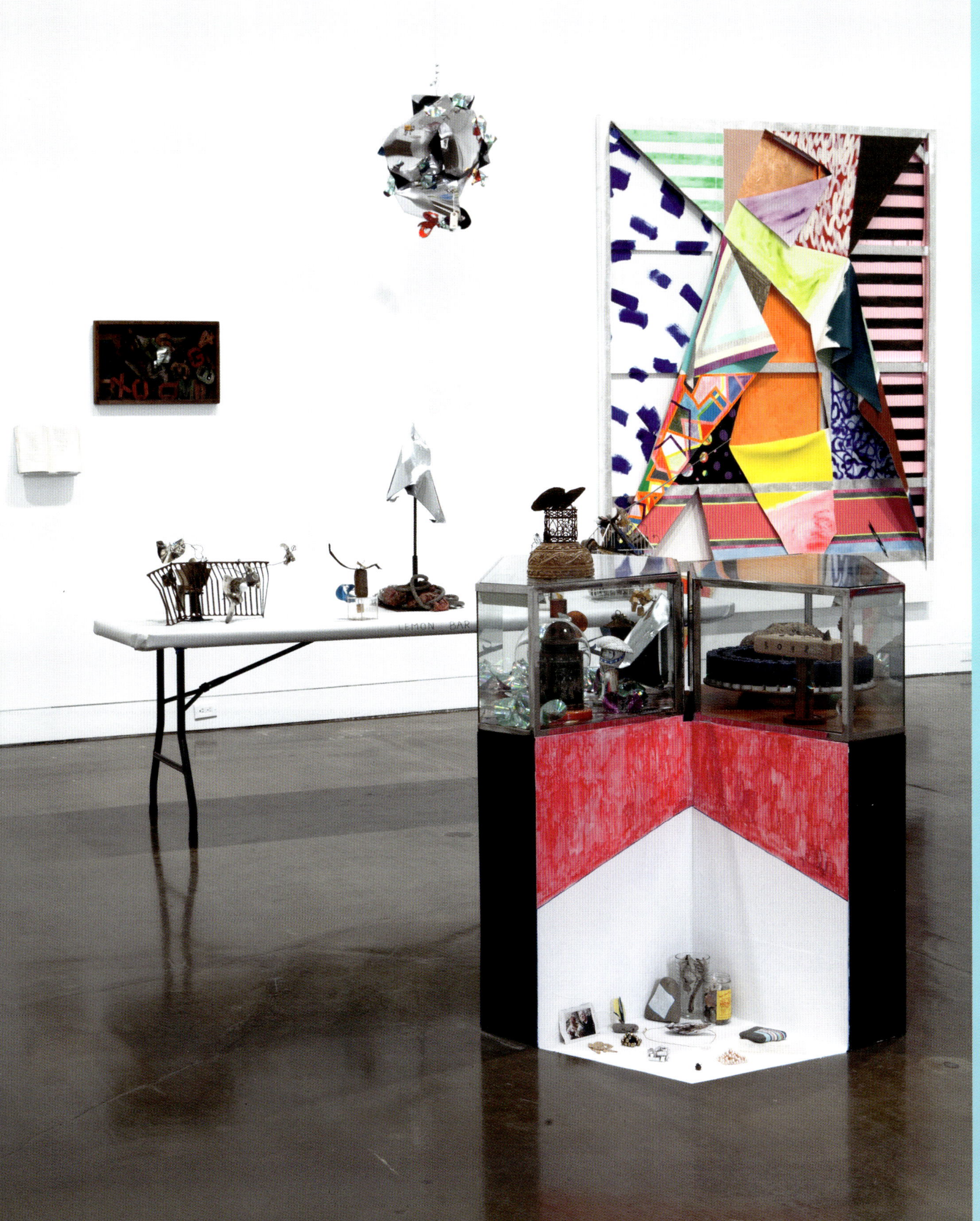
LEMON BAR

OF
GALAXIES

MANTLE

SANITY
CHECK

bounced: insufficient funds

DYNAMICS
OF
SMALL
MAMMALS

THE EQUIVAL
UN

EARLY
RIPPLES

HYSICAL OCEANOGRAPHY

EORETICAL STUDIES

THE PLOT
OF
INTENSITY

CONTINENTAL
TECTONICS

COMPLEXITY
THEORISTS

THE
GLISSANDO
OF
LIFE

THE BUBB
OF THE E

TIME IS CURVED

Sarah Cain and George Herms

Interview by Sarah C. Bancroft

Sarah Cain and George Herms
Installation of handwritten titles on paper pattern pieces on the side of the *Dos Quesadillas* display cases (detail)

SB: You knew each other before I paired you in this exhibition; tell me about your history.

SC: I was lucky enough to be at Skowhegan when George was there in 2006. My studio was right next door to his. When George came over to the studio, we were instantly on the same wavelength. I was dealing a lot with the idea of the unknown, abstraction, the difficulties of language within what I am doing, so it was just like meeting a kindred spirit. We could *not* talk about the difficulties of language; I mean, we could have a language without a language and understand it. So that was a great intro to our friendship.

GH: I think of wanting to bridge the language and the visual arts and yet not wanting to. We're ambivalent about it: we do talk—we're talking right now—but that's why that poem of Duncan McNaughton's that we are including in our installation is so important. He starts it off with the conquistadors, talking about language, letters: "the conquest, of words, of speech, of all we have been capable of saying, by letters, los conquistadores." (I love "los conquistadores" and the corral "of sounds and letters.") I think you and I struggle with this to this very day. I found out there's something called speciphobia, which is fear of specifics. [*Laughter.*]

SB: Previously you mentioned a discussion at Skowhegan about the frustration of using concrete language to describe abstraction. Can you talk about that a little more?

SC: Language is frequently used to tell viewers what they are experiencing. I've always gravitated toward abstraction for the openness that it allows. I use it in a way similar to the space between a hypothesis and a conclusion; it is an experimental free zone.

SB: Was there anxiety over being asked what your work meant and how to define it?

SC: Not really anxiety, just the need to resist limitations. I never set out to make an artwork knowing what it'll end up being; I don't see the point in doing what is already known. The process is about discovery, freedom, and the evolution of thoughts.

GH: That's that loyalty to the shaping principle within a work because you don't sit on it with an architect's blueprint when you go to work. So that frees one up. You know, it can be scary. The great Bill Evans, the piano player, said you can go just so far on intuition and then you need knowledge. Otherwise you can get hung out to dry. So one does need to be able to talk about it. But I never went to art school until, finally, at Cal State Fullerton, I started teaching [*laughter*] and was amazed that they had on the side of the building "Visual Art." And after a month or two I wanted to go and change it to "Verbal Arts" because this was '78 or something and conceptual art was coming on like gangbusters. And people were telling me these incredible things, but I said, "Yeah, but it's not on the canvas, man." So that kind of situation, people having to defend themselves, the critique situation, I have never been through that; I can't take any criticism. The hair on the back of my neck goes up because I don't know what I'm doing. I've never been able to have a studio assistant because I don't know what I'm going to be doing, you know. Maybe "that long two-by-four, you can go get the other end and lift it" or something. [*Laughter.*]

SB: You often don't have to know what you're doing in order to make relevant work.

SC: Right, I allow myself the state of not knowing. Although it's very possible that I do know what I'm doing, but I think the unknown allows better results as well as introducing chance, which is a principle all three of us employ in our work.

I've always struggled with the person who talks well but doesn't make great work having the power of persuasive words. And then the opposite is true for great work that can't be easily co-opted into a narrative. I struggle with how to translate into language to someone who is rushing through the looking process.

SB: It's the work that communicates when the person doesn't have the skills. Other times the person is much stronger than the work, which isn't a good thing either.

GH: You're dealt a hand. Verbal skills and visual skills don't always come in the same hand.

SC: Yeah, and verbal and visual skills don't always come at the same time. When I met George, I was really spinning out from this. I frequently remember the metaphor George used in our first meeting: being in your practice is a spiral moving inward, but being an artist in the world is an outward spiral, and getting caught between the two can be tricky. I was just out of grad school and coming from San Francisco, where being an abstract painter really was not cool. I had to defend it. But it's so much easier here. I don't know whether it's just because I'm in a bigger city and there are more people and space, or if it's timing, but I have found that I don't have to defend so much anymore.

GH: They're still talking about L.A. as a place where you can have that freedom to experiment today.

SC: Is it just because of the space here?

GH: It's the hierarchy. There isn't the hierarchy. Everybody wants to say, "Let's make it a big city," but it's all these small towns that just grew together.

Another thing, somehow San Francisco is like roots for both of us. And yet meeting in Skowhegan there was no real geographical sense; we were just all in the woods in Maine. The other thing you need to credit in this exhibition is the weaving of generations. It's so healthy, and it's our future.

SB: And it's not every artist who is interested in recognizing younger artists (teachers being an exception).

SC: I'm thankful I've always had people twice my age that I've talked to regularly. George is very generous, open, and curious. A lot of artists are not generous with each other.

GH: Jazz musicians I celebrate in my opera—Bobby Bradford, John Carter, and Horace Tapscott—they all have under their wings younger musicians coming up. In the visual arts, we should have this going on as well. I mean, face it, I came out of nowhere. Charles Brittin, the photographer, he said I was a complete enigma when I hit the scene. [*Laughter.*] All of a sudden on my twentieth birthday, in Topanga, right down from where I am now, Wallace Berman and Bob Alexander walked into my life, and I followed them back into Los Angeles and what eventually became the Beat generation. Most of those people were ten years older than I was, and they were in full stride, so I just started emulating them. They were very generous with me and patient, and I didn't have to talk until I was thirty, which was very cool because they all had something to say.

You know, I would go teach every seven years for one year (the opposite of taking a sabbatical). I never got caught in that academic thing. So it was a level playing field; we're all in this together, and no one has special purchase on all that knowledge or wisdom.

SB: Talk to me about the use of text in your project.

GH: Once you get a Guggenheim Fellowship, they send you a pamphlet each year of who got a Guggenheim. Here's some titles of fellows' research papers: "Dynamics of small mammals," "Repetition and difference in Homer," "Theoretical studies in physical oceanography," "Control of insect metamorphoses." I suggested that we could use these as titles for pieces, and so I copied them out and we each have a copy of these. Some of them seem to me to have something to do with painting.

"Early ripples"—that would be a good painting title. So it's letting the language… it's like found-object art but instead it's found phrases, found language.

SC: Found languages. We both get into experimentation with words; I think it has to do with a Beat appreciation of words. Bill Berkson, a really important mentor and mutual friend, introduced me to another dear friend, Bernadette Mayer. She is a cult figure in experimental poetry. She and Bill helped shape my sense of freedom with words. Actually, Bill showed me a work of George's in his home with Connie Lewallen, years before I met George. Poets surround you too, George; both of us had the luxury of growing up with poets around.

GH: Well, those are the artists of language; their art is language.

SC: The abstract artists of language.

GH: When I used the LOVE Press to print books of poetry, the way the words are on a page, it's almost like Charlie Parker's music. The spaces between the notes are almost as important as the notes. One of the books that I published was by Michael McClure, and he had one of those typewriters that had a very small typeface so he could write a really long line. And here's Diane di Prima and Berman sitting around with me, like, "What can we have George do?" [*Laughter.*] "What about this poem of Michael's?" So I rebuilt it so that the lines were completely long instead of broken. I sent it to Michael, and he said, you know, "That's exactly the way I wrote it." That length of line was his voice. It's the breath; your line is a breath. So the ear and the eye are one in the heart. That's my position. And then there are works of art that sing, that make your heart sing when you stand in front of them. So this is the goal I would set for myself: after hearing poets read or leaving a jazz club after hearing musicians play, you're like about three feet off the ground and *so* glad to be a human being, that this is our species. So that's always what I wanted from any exhibition.

SC: That's a good goal.

SB: How are you working together on your project for this exhibition?

GH: The first step was to go and view the space.

SC: Even before that, I came down to see you, and you handed me the *Scientific American* with words and jargon underlined. So that was the first thing; it started with abstracted language. Neither of us has collaborated with another artist, so it has been a really cool learning experience. How to improvise together, follow the lead and be flexible, and the idea of an arc between our practices developed, and then that became a composition. I think we've just been introducing things to each other and seeing if they stick.

GH: It's very much like a Ping-Pong game. I throw something at you, and you absorb it and take what you can use, and then you throw something back at me. And your bounce back to me always seems to be something that I find nourishing and I can use. So there's been no real editing process at this point, just a smorgasbord of ideas.

SB: So you're each presenting individual works, but there is this dialogue through the titles in the installation.

SC: Well, there's a dialogue through a lot of things—I mean, if it works out that the work on-site *works*. [*Laughter.*] The painting that moves from the wall to the floor will visually bring the objects together. You know, I feel the text is the same as paint or a color; I don't think it's too different.

GH: I think that the language part has more quantity, but the same process has gone on visually. I believe it's based on our knowing what the other artist is capable of and an appreciation. I saw that space as being transformed by Sarah, and then I'm bringing in my display cases (now called *Dos Quesadillas*) and dropping them in. So all of these things have just been like assemblage. It's an additive process.

SC: Yeah, it's the key between us. I think for both of us, what we do, it's collage, whether it's words or space.

GH: That's the medium.

SB: When I originally asked whether you'd work together, George said he would "corroborate" rather than collaborate.

GH: *Corroborate*, yeah, I like that word better.

SB: It's like corroborating each other's practices but also the joint project.

SC: Yeah, which is great because I have never made anything collaboratively. It's really intense, but I have learned. I'm working on a proposal with another artist now, and I never would have said yes to it if it had happened before this. So it's been a good learning experience and understanding, too, that both of us are solo agents.

GH: Yeah, and neither of us is really interested in convincing the other one of shit. [*Laughter.*]

SB: Tell me about the physical installation as you see it now.

SC: I'm going to show two paintings and a work on paper. Then a third canvas will come out perpendicular to the wall and act as a false wall to start the arc and activate the space. I'm going to pick up on some of the paint that moves through the first canvas and extend that out on the wall and floor to create this arc over and through our corner. George will drop in some sculptures, and I will work compositionally with the shapes within his works or the support structures and hopefully make an environment that the viewer can walk inside and just sort of cohesively bring it together.

GH: This piece will have finite components like the paintings she mentions, and what I will be doing is dropping in display cases in the middle of the floor and the *Lemon Bar* in the middle. I make sculptures that fall over; I have thoughts that fly away and a third one I'm ashamed of, but it's fear of running out of sugar. So anyway, sculptures that fall over, that's my signature style. Any sculpture that doesn't fall over, that's a "lemon," right? So that's the *Lemon Bar*: it's only going to have sculptures that stand up. These sculptures come in—and I'm waving my arms around, which is difficult for the tape recorder to catch—and there's this arc of space like a pond. Our works will be drawn together; my sculptures will be dropped in, and the ripples that go out from my work are what you [Sarah Cain] are going to be picking up on.

SB: Anything else you want to talk about?

GH: There should be a toast to "Continental tectonics." We already did "Repetition and difference." "The bubble-like surfaces of the enormous void," that's the one I thought Sarah should be working on. I'll be working on "Sheet of galaxies." "The grasp of the condition"—neither one of us is in shape to do that. [*Laughter.*] Anyway, we're having so much fun, Sarah.

Overleaf:
Sarah Cain and George Herms
Korral, 2011 (installation view)

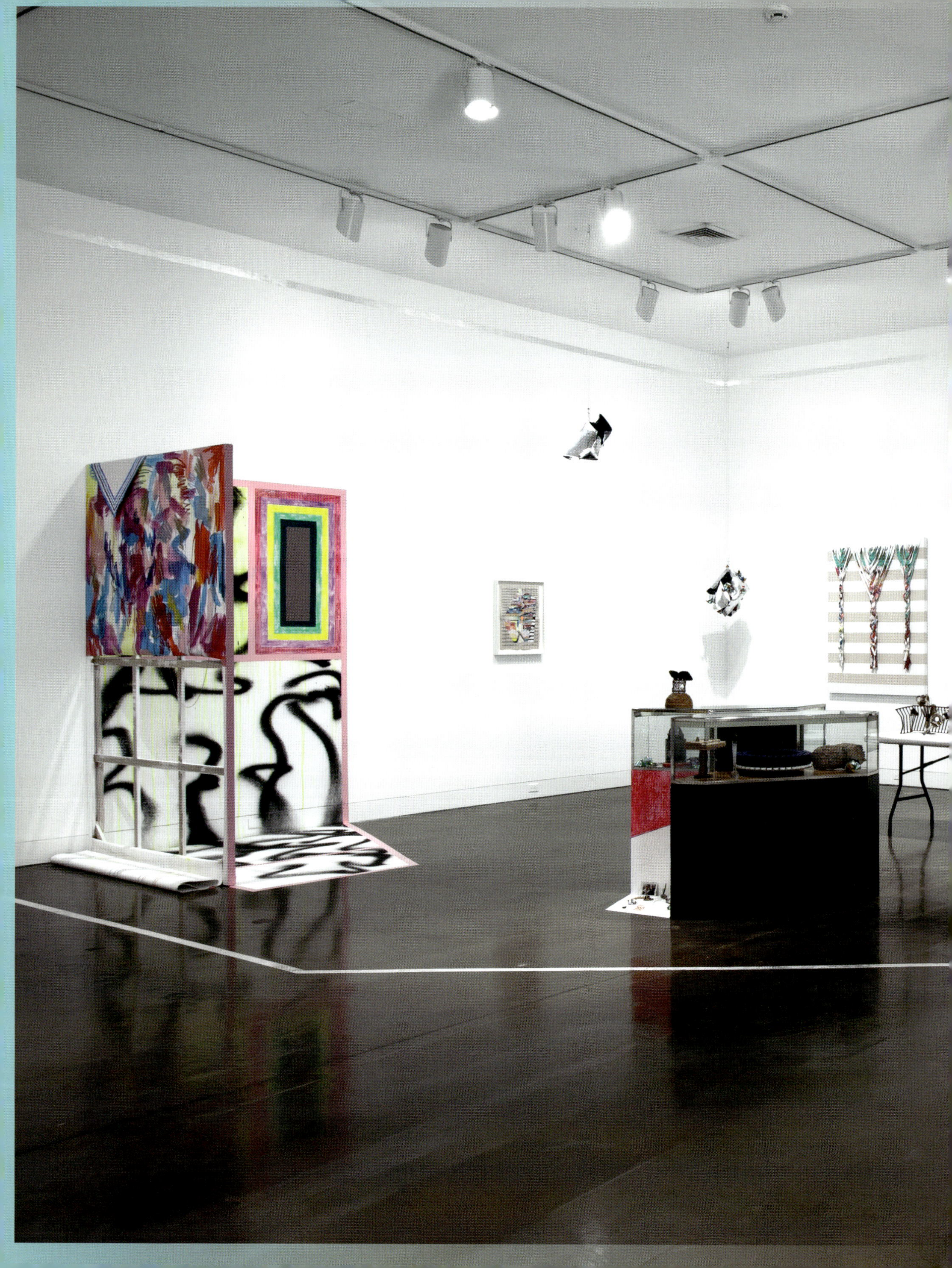

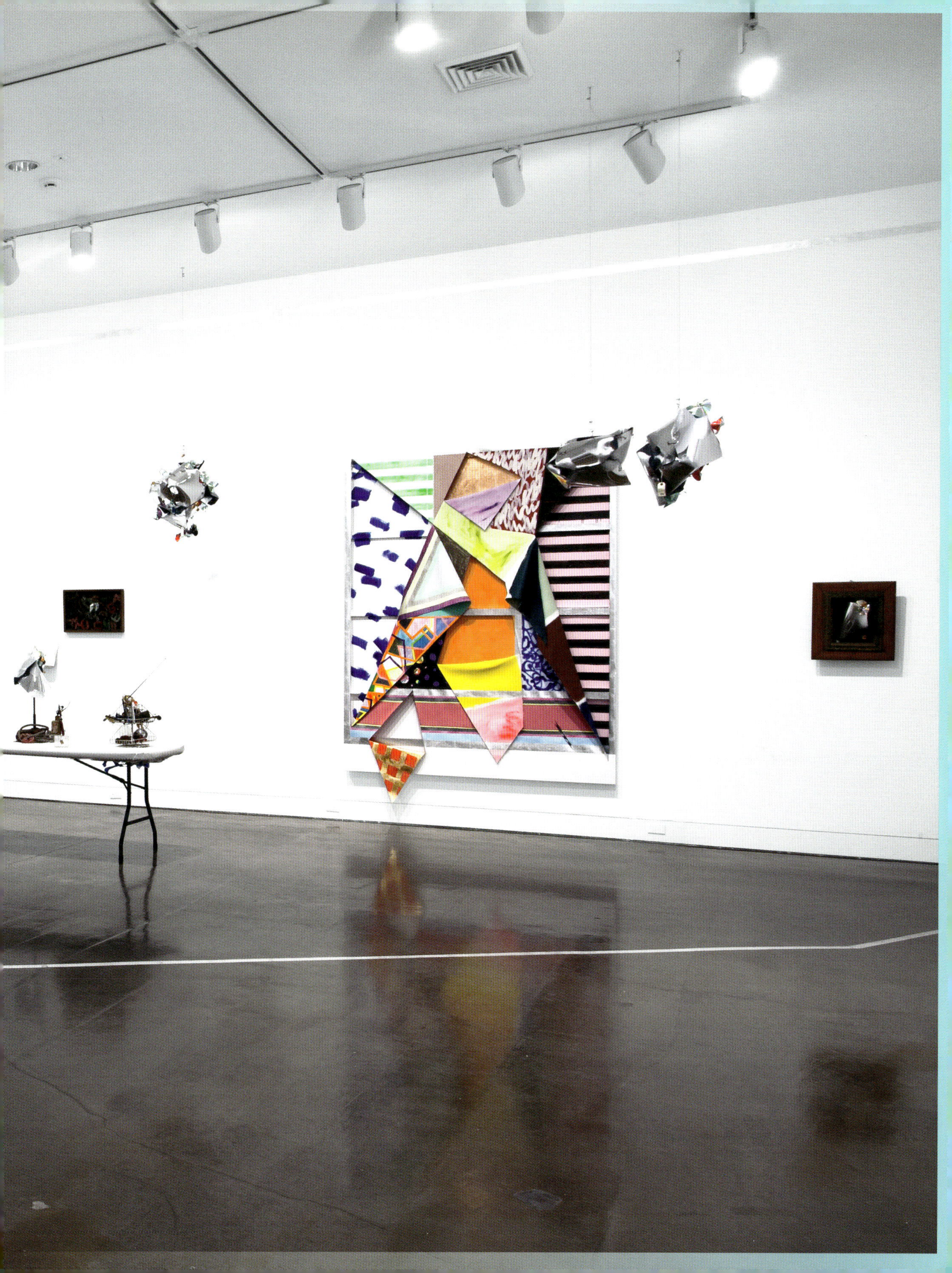

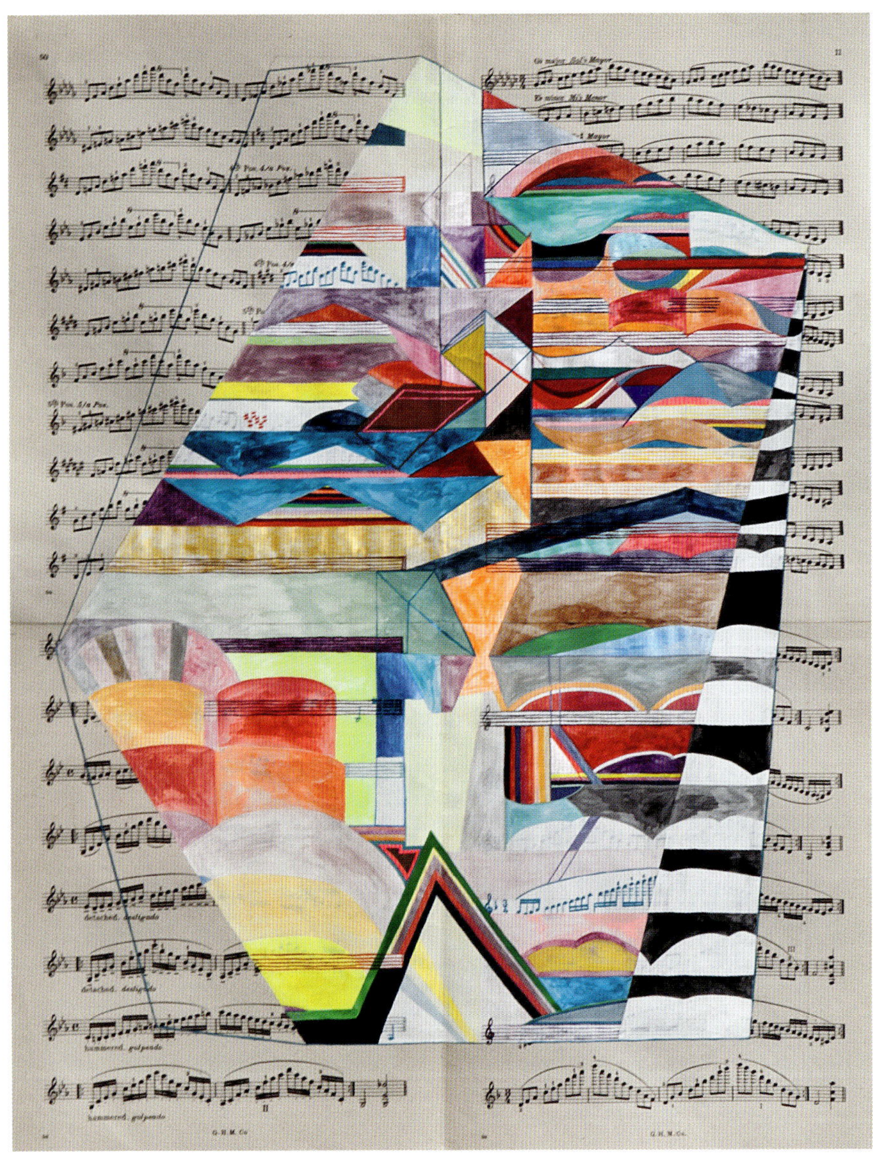

Sarah Cain
Untitled (Strings), 2010

Sarah Cain and George Herms
Korral, 2011 (installation view)
Foreground: George Herms, *Lemon Bar* installation, with (left to right): *Lemon Bar (Untitled Wood Paddle)*, 2011; *Lemon Bar (Song)*, 2011; *Lemon Bar (Centerpiece)*, 2011; *Lemon Bar (P.R.)*, 2011; *Lemon Bar (Beyond H. D.)*, 2011
Background: George Herms, *BBQ MoonRock #3*, 2011 (suspended); Sarah Cain, *French Braid*, 2011 (on wall)

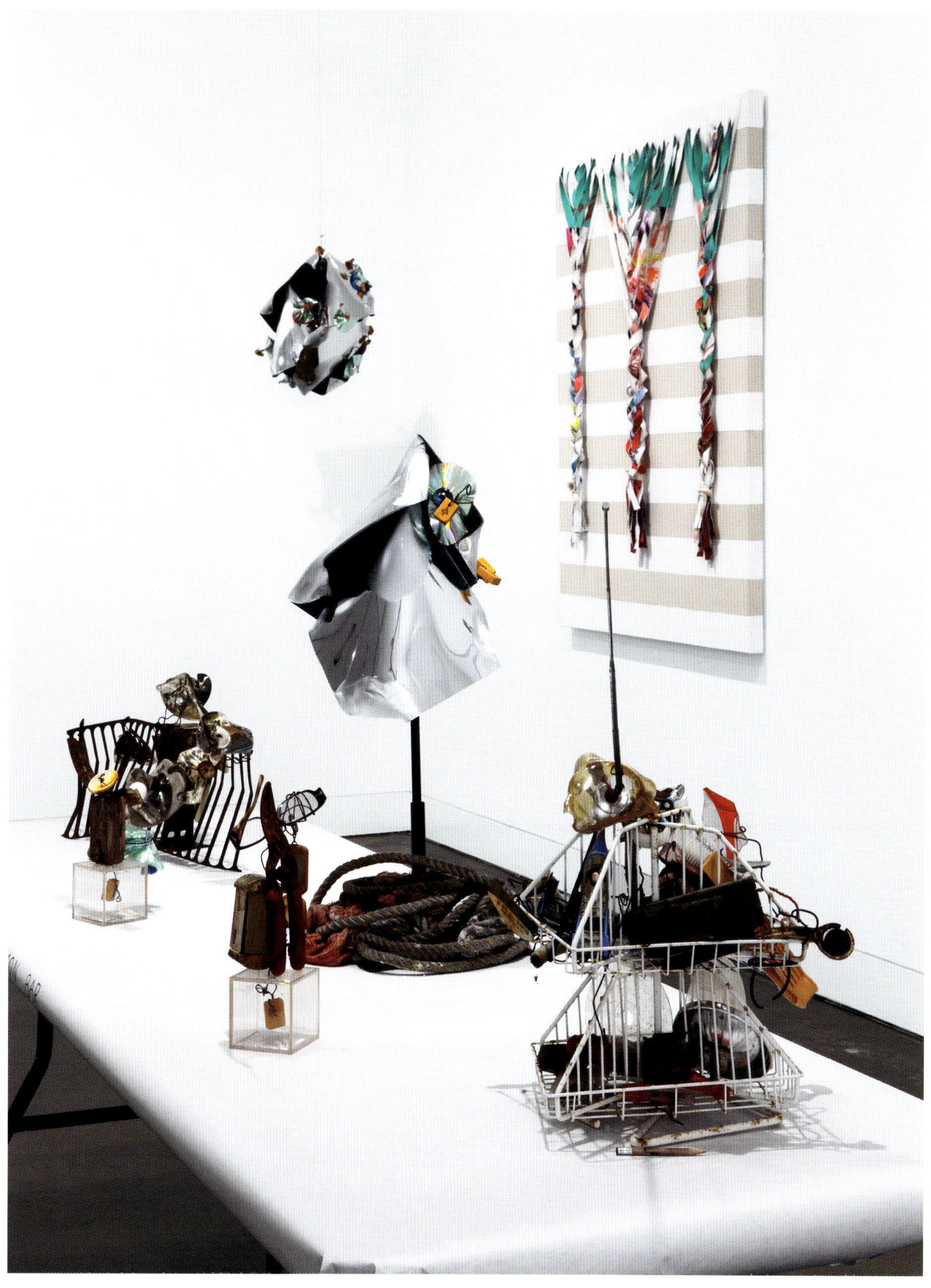

George Herms
Me and Mrs. Jones, 2011

George Herms's copy of Duncan McNaughton's book *Capricci* (Bolinas, CA: Blue Millennium Press, 2003), opened to the poem "Me and Mrs. Jones"

Sarah Cain
Untitled (Spring 2011), 2011
(installation view, artist's studio)

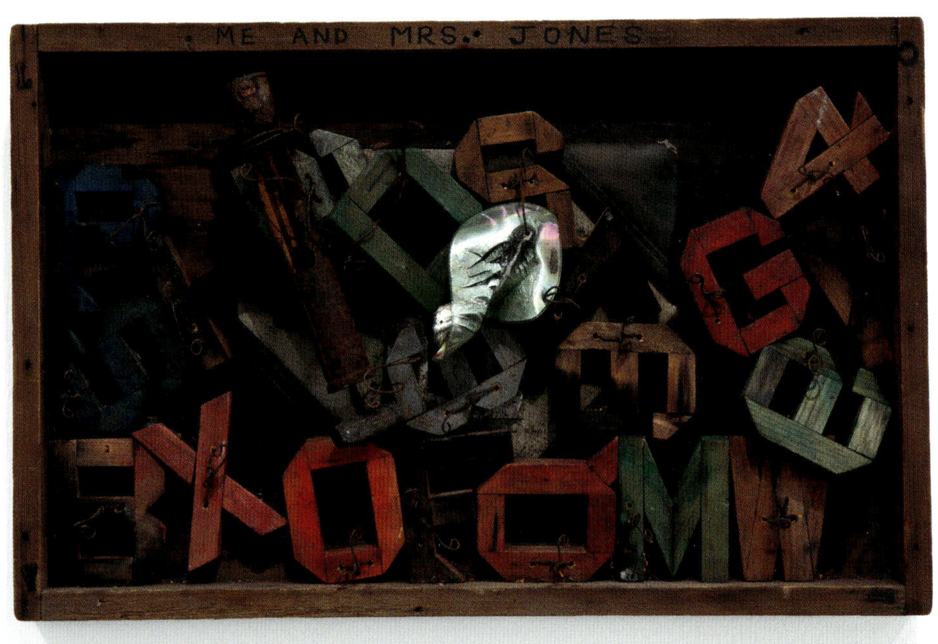

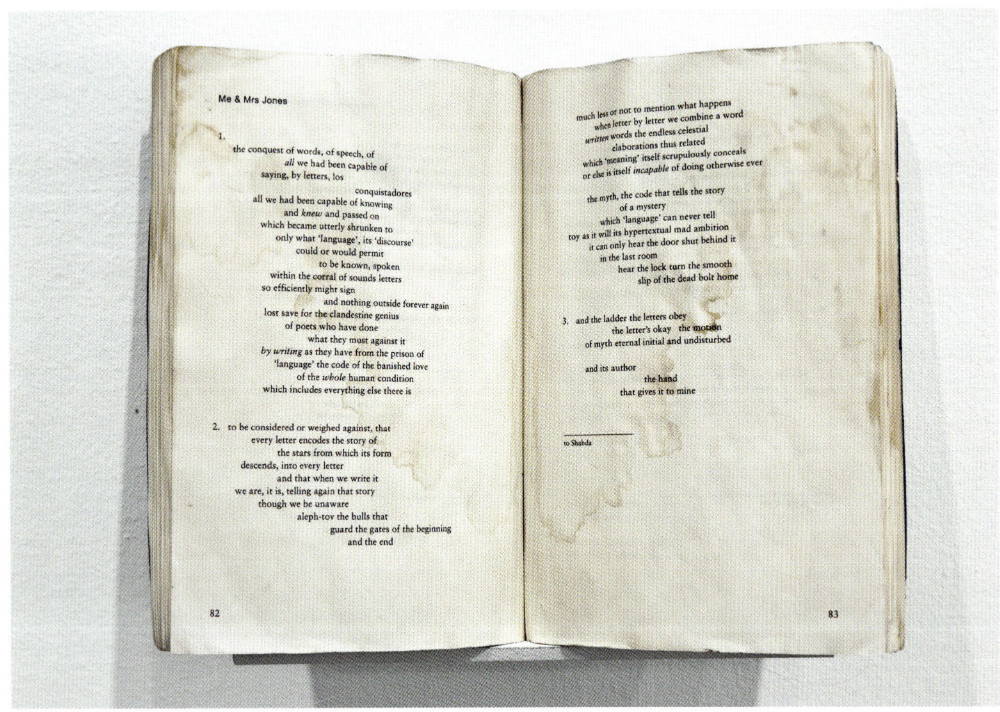

Me & Mrs Jones

1.
the conquest of words, of speech, of
all we had been capable of
saying, by letters, los
conquistadores
all we had been capable of knowing
and *knew* and passed on
which became utterly shrunken to
only what 'language', its 'discourse'
could or would permit
to be known, spoken
within the corral of sounds letters
so efficiently might sign
and nothing outside forever again
lost save for the clandestine genius
of poets who have done
what they must against it
by writing as they have from the prison of
'language' the code of the banished love
of the *whole* human condition
which includes everything else there is

2. to be considered or weighed against, that
every letter encodes the story of
the stars from which its form
descends, into every letter
and that when we write it
we are, it is, telling again that story
though we be unaware
aleph-tov the bulls that
guard the gates of the beginning
and the end

82

much less or not to mention what happens
when letter by letter we combine a word
written words the endless celestial
elaborations thus related
which 'meaning' itself scrupulously conceals
or else is itself *incapable* of doing otherwise ever

the myth, the code that tells the story
of a mystery
which 'language' can never tell
toy as it will its hypertextual mad ambition
it can only hear the door shut behind it
in the last room
hear the lock turn the smooth
slip of the dead bolt home

3. and the ladder the letters obey
the letter's okay the motion
of myth eternal initial and undisturbed

and its author
the hand
that gives it to mine

---
to Shabda

83

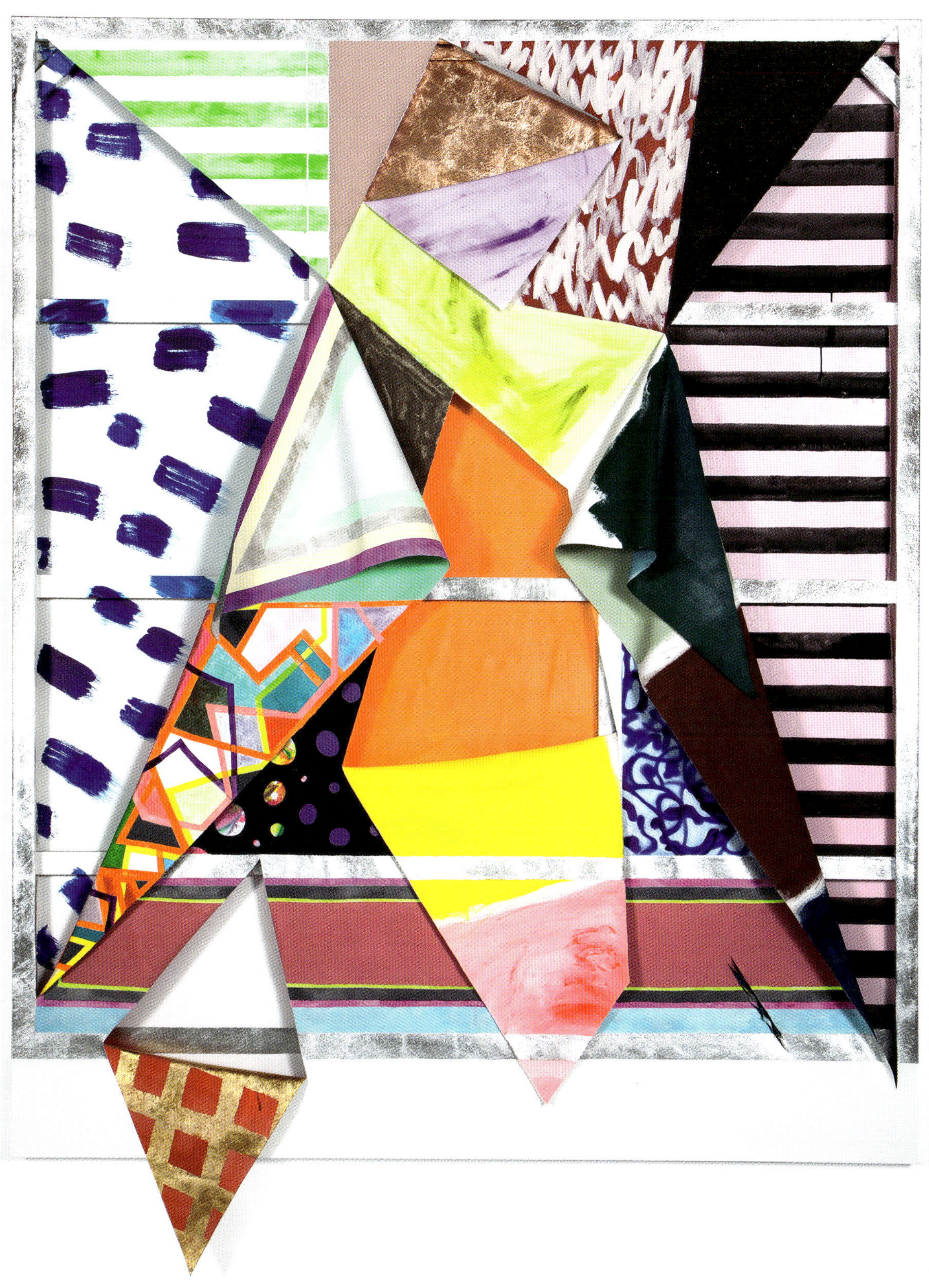

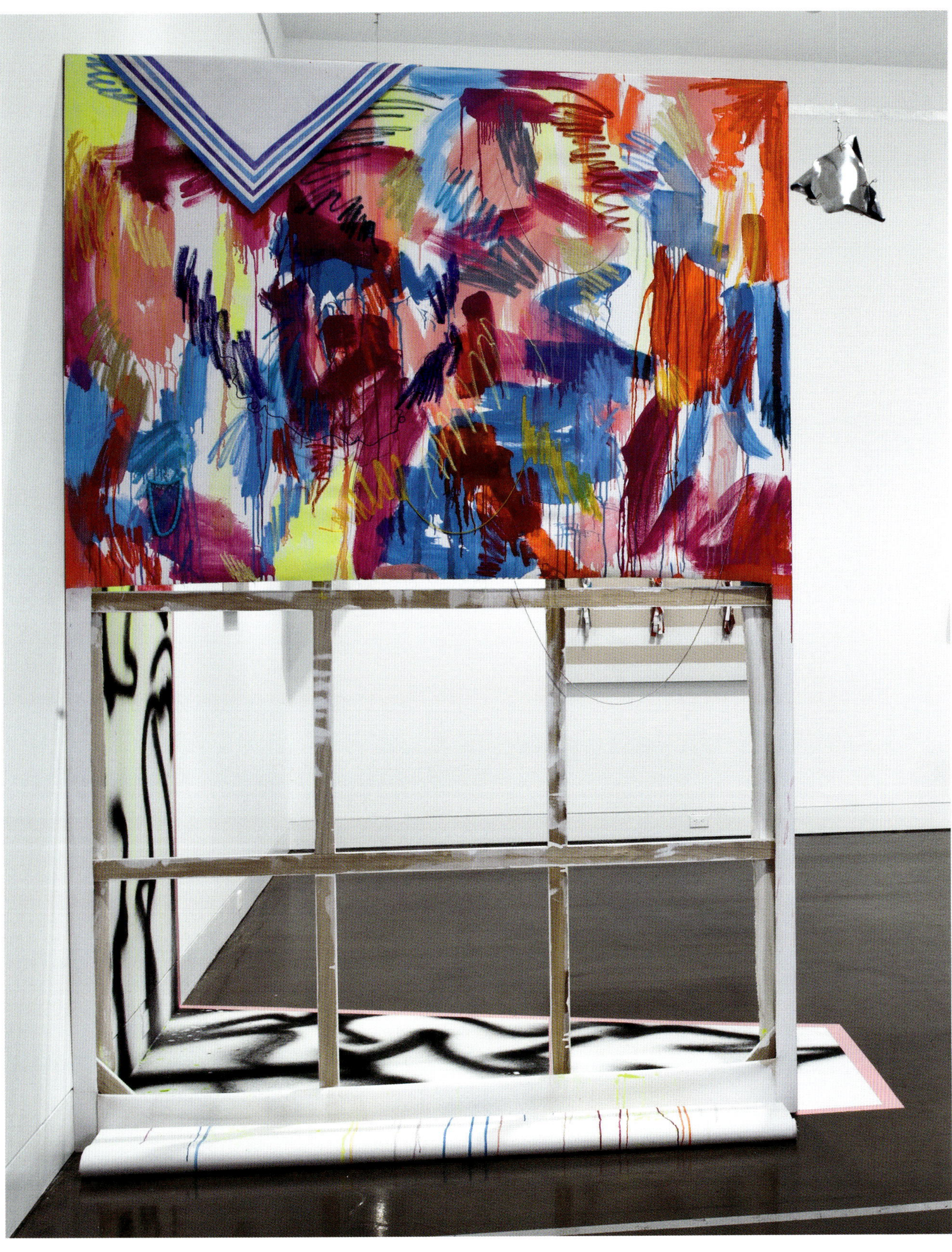

Sarah Cain
Untitled (Fall 2011), 2011
(installation view)

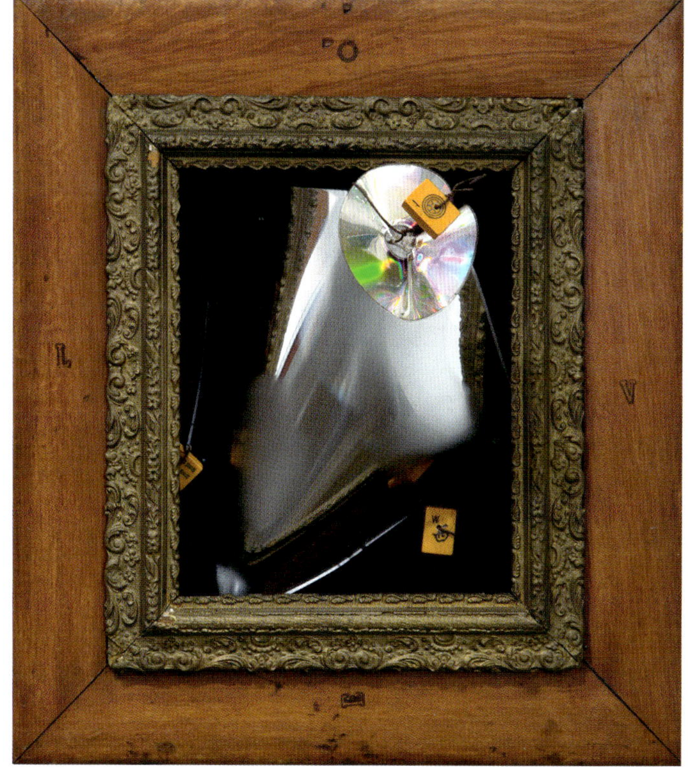

"In attempting to understand the arts objectively I am searching for general truths. The effect of this enforced intellectualization on my painting, however, is just the opposite from what one might expect. Research skims off the purely cerebral, leaving for the studio those layers of consciousness (for which we have no effective label) that lie between the intellect and the unconscious. The median area is freed from the straightjacket of formation and verbalization, so that one can paint without intellectualized thoughts. The responses to the subject and the medium which govern the growth of the picture are *felt* convictions, not at all subject to the scrutiny of logic. But the fact that the artist paints in what seems to be an automatic manner does not in the least imply that his theories, his ethics, his ideals, and his cynicisms, are not involved. The more he can both broaden and intensify his knowledge, empathy, and cognizance of the world and himself, the richer is the raw material which gives meaning to his paintings. I cannot believe that the humanist scholar and the artist must, by definition, be separate. The barrier which has arisen between their twin approaches toward the truths of existence is one of the sad phenomena of modern life. Intellect, emotion, and sense need not be separated." *

From a letter sent by Bill Seitz in the early '50s to Marion Willard, his dealer in New York, as quoted in the introduction to [title, date etc. of Seitz exhibition catalog].

Sarah: * This is what we began in Skowhegan

George Herms, *Seitz*, 2011

Sarah Cain and George Herms, *From a letter sent by Bill Seitz in the early 50s to Marion Willard, his art dealer in New York . . .*, 2011

STANYA KAHN AND LLYN FOULKES *HAPPY SONG FOR YOU,* 2011

Stanya Kahn and Llyn Foulkes merge their mutual interests in performance, improvisation, sound making, the horrific, and humor in this collaborative project.

Stanya Kahn and Llyn Foulkes
Happy Song for You, 2011 (installation view)

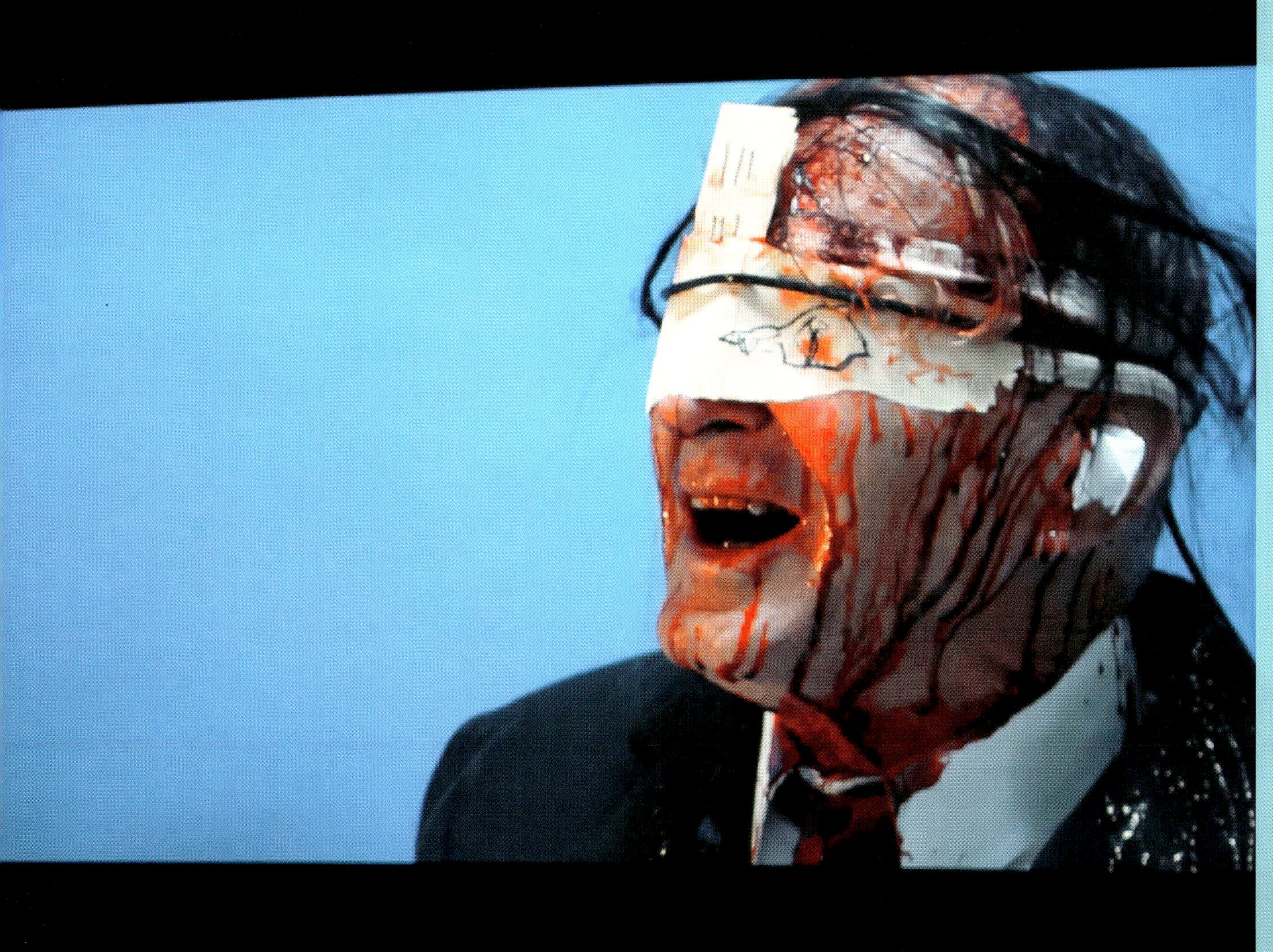

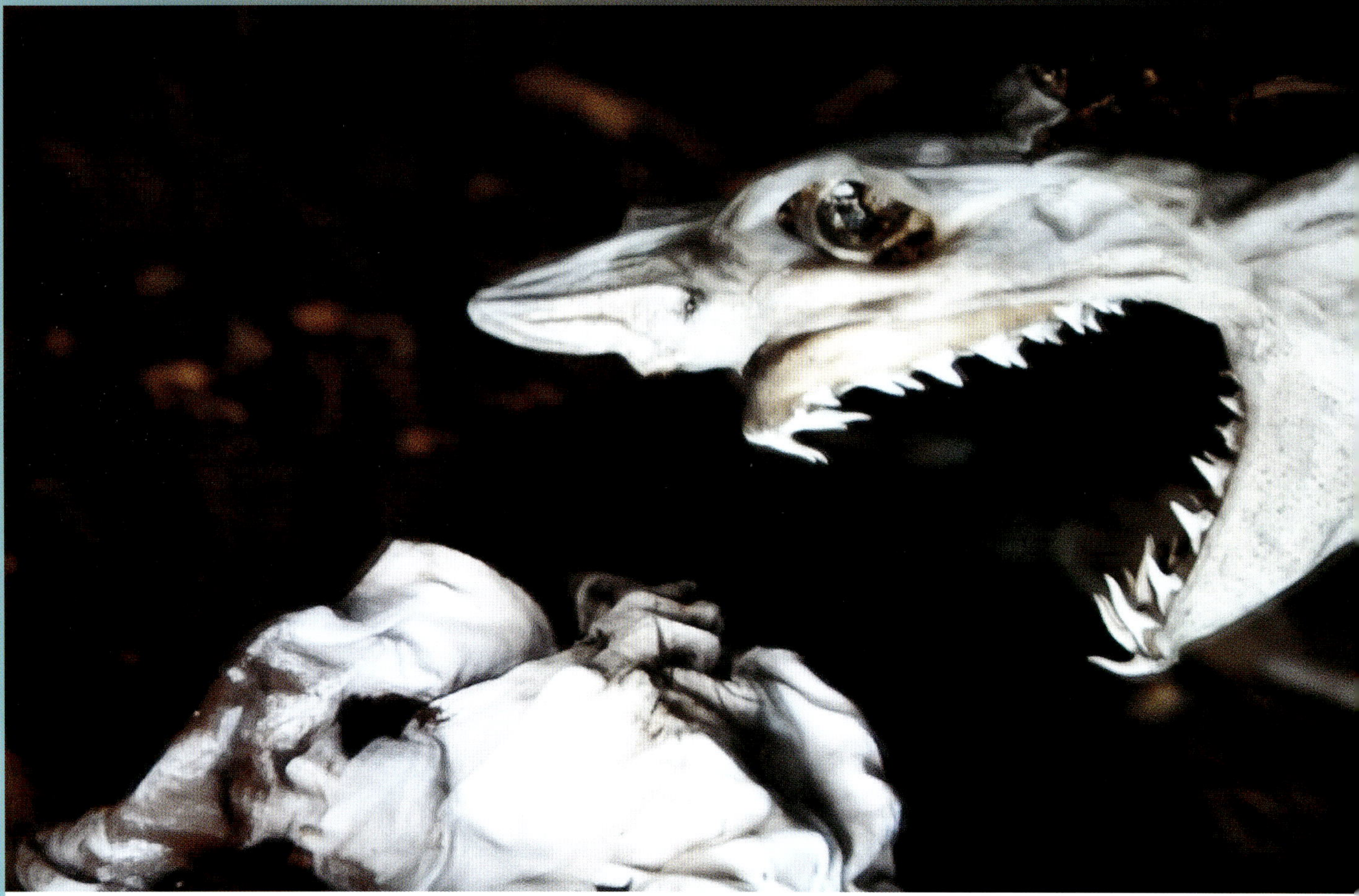

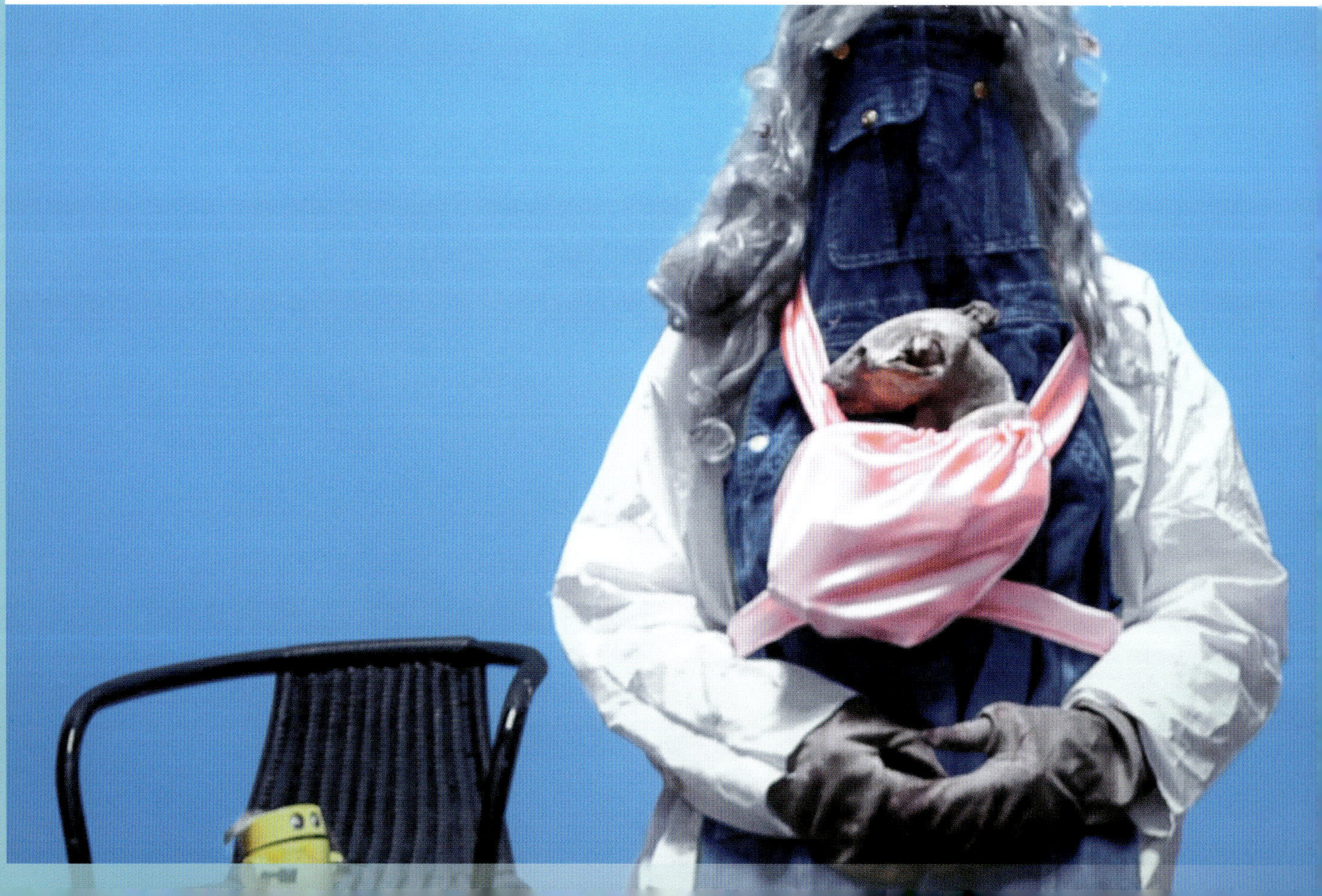

Stanya Kahn and Llyn Foulkes

Interview by Catherine Taft

Stanya Kahn and Llyn Foulkes
Stills from *Happy Song for You*, 2011

CT: You have both created work collaboratively in the past, with either a band or a partner, yet you eventually made a choice to create on your own. Now you are collaborating again, and I just had the chance to see the first videos you made together. I'm curious about how that process began. Did it take some time to get going?

SK: One of the things that is cool about our getting to know each other is that we relate artist to artist, but I also feel a generational difference. I find myself saying, "Stanya, shut up and listen because Llyn's got three times more life experience than you." As an artist, he's been making work so much longer than I have, and it's really good to be around someone who has thought a lot about process.

LF: Working with Stanya, I think about how I was thirty years ago, and those experiences are still coming back. There's a certain kind of energy and creativity that you have at that age that moves faster. And when you get old, you start thinking about life a little more, and I get into the deep things more now. Except when I'm playing on the Machine [Foulkes's sculptural instrument used in his one-man band]; then I can be really spontaneous, and I could even get up and dance. It's a place that brings me back to my youth. And when I'm off the Machine, I'm just this old guy. So yeah, there's a generational thing. And I think Stanya is really creative, and I like where she's coming from, and we can identify on that level.

CT: You are each so skilled with improvisation. When you began working, how much did you plan ahead—individually or together—and how much was improvised? When did that decision happen?

LF: Well, kind of at the same time. I saw some of her drawings of these masks, and we decided to make them. We went down to a wig place to get materials and look at stuff, and then it went really fast. Stanya spent hours sewing hair onto these masks, then we had to do our thinking right on the spot and go shoot with the masks. So it happened at the same time. From the start, I thought I wanted to make a mystery. The idea of keeping a person wondering is always good. But we're still working now, so the piece is kind of a mystery already. [*Laughter.*]

SK: As part of our process, one of the main things we talk about is the different ways of working: the difference between making a map and setting out to execute it or finding it as we go. This is similar to how I've heard you talk about your paintings, Llyn. You don't exactly make a big plan and execute it.

LF: No, they usually just turn into something like faces. When I started to paint the big rocks back in the 1960s, I pressed rags into paint and saw heads emerge. So there's a connection there. I was intrigued by a film I saw of Stanya's and that the people in it become weird. And since she is a video person, I just let her lead me around.

SK: And you have quite a bit of input too. Remember the first day in the basement? Going down to the basement to shoot evolved out of our talking, but we both organically started seeing faces in objects down there.

LF: Yes, that went to my heart in a way. It was very cool. And we were talking about how sounds might come out of these faces.

SK: It was cool because we were seeing them at the same time. And then my brain—as a moving-pictures brain—started thinking about how we could get things moving outside.

CT: What I love about this footage is that at a certain point, Llyn, you come out with a dried, shriveled shark head, and you make that interact with the other found objects. Had you planned to bring that with you to the shoot?

LF: Yes, and a dried dead dog.

SK: It was great! So you brought creepy dead guys…

LF: Well, I've got a lot of creepy stuff.

SK: And I picked a "creepy dead guy" location in the basement, so it worked out.

LF: That was a creepy basement. There might be a body buried in that dirt. There's our mystery!

CT: It's interesting that you started out on this micro level, looking very closely, and then you stepped back and entered into the landscape with animals, vistas, and using your own bodies. Can we talk about your different notions of performance as it relates to your two practices?

LF: We're coming from different places.

SK: But what we share in common is that we both love a lot of physical comedy and comedians.

LF: And also an interest in the horrific. My concept of the horrific came from the wars and reflecting on man's inhumanity toward man.

SK: Mine feels related to that, but it also ties in to a personal sense of distress. I try to find a way of externalizing that with humor but still with some darkness and gore. I think we share a sense of personal disaster constantly mirroring back the big-picture disaster. I identified that in your paintings when I first saw them and I could relate to it.

CT: When I heard about this collaboration, it made sense to me. You both seem to construct representations of failure, although you do it in very different ways. Llyn, you make very clear critiques of American consumerism, and your songs are often about broken dreams. Stanya, it's much more subtle in your work, but it's there. You present wounded characters who just wander through these American wastelands.

LF: I'm a populist, and I've been through it. I've always been anticommercial. There's a whole structure that has to do with money, and it's ruining our society. How do you get around that? I work through those ideas with my Machine. With songs like "I'm Afraid I'm Not Gonna Make It."

SK: Maybe we share the feeling that what society sees as failure is actually a productive space; it's outside of the standards and those categories of success or status. Yet I think my work is about resistance. My "characters" are resilient. They continue to form jokes and travel across the land when their exteriors are symbolizing the broken, the yucky and injured. They signify damage, but in that state they almost become free. And through a relentless joking, there's another machine that's running.

CT: Another connection I see in your bodies of work—and I think this relates to how you each approach performance—is the way that a "self" is created but also defaced.

LF: Sometimes it is me in my work. The first bloody head painting I made in the 1970s was me. It was called *Who Is on Third?* I had seen an autopsy where the scalp was pulled down over the front of a face. That was the feeling combined with Buster Keaton saying that he could throw a cream pie from the pitcher's mound and hit a man in the face running from second to third. But I've always identified with my work. As a little boy I was spoiled by my grandmother. I was the center of the universe, and that just played out. That's probably how I wound up being a one-man band. I had to control every aspect.

SK: I'm always displacing myself. You're not supposed to look at my work and say, "That's Stanya." Before I came to video, I was making one-person performances that I wrote, directed, and made sets for and did the sound, lighting, and costumes. I had total control. A lot of that content was drawn from my own experiences, but it was never recast to be an image of myself. And there was always some version of masking, whether it was with broken glasses or hats. There was always a displacement. The word *self* is murky. My hope is always that even the person that I am on-screen is somehow relatable; I want the viewers to project themselves into that space somehow.

CT: But Llyn, it seems like you're comfortable letting your own psychology enter into the space of your work?

LF: My own psychology? I don't know. For this piece I just wanted to make a film and put music to it. There was some disconnect about how we would use sound. I wanted to play music on my Machine, but then Stanya found all of these electronic sounds. I know where she's coming from, but I know it's a computer program, and I have a certain kind of precious quality about making my own sounds.

SK: I feel similarly about how I work with sound. I'm not just only taking prerecorded sounds from an effects library online. I'm changing them and sometimes making my own sounds. I also have an old-fashioned work ethos about using sounds from material I made. For example, I recorded you walking through the grass yesterday, and to me there is integrity in using the particular sound that your body made. The disconnect might have something to do with this idea of displacing something farther or closer. I take normal sounds and turn them into another sound, just like I source from myself to create a different persona.

CT: What I hear you both saying—which is really interesting to me, and may result from a generational difference—is that you're both after authenticity, but it's two very different versions of the authentic.

LF: Yes, Stanya's taking her life and her sounds and making them flexible, as I am. I need a lot of control with my sounds because I am performing them with my whole body. Growing up, my idol was Chaplin. He directed his movies; he acted; he did the music. So maybe it makes sense that now I am a one-man band.

SK: Chaplin, Buster Keaton, Jerry Lewis, so many of the great comedians wrote, directed, and controlled their productions because they knew how they wanted them to go. They innately understood the timing of their own performativity and the environment they needed to make that happen. And I respect that. That's what's funny about us coming together and why we needed to start from scratch with our piece.

LF: Exactly. We're very alike in this way. But I would never want to be like those actors and do an hour and a half of makeup.

SK: But I do it for my own work. In my last piece I was totally bandaged with prosthetics. I had wood strapped to my leg and both hands bandaged. I was completely disabled.

LF: Did it have to be you?

SK: Of course it had to be me. Who else would it be? It couldn't be someone else playing Chaplin. He had to do it. Even the best comedians stay in control all the time. Lucille Ball ran her entire show.

CT: You both have a shared passion for comedy and these different tropes that exist in popular culture. I wondered if either of you has a conscious relationship to performing genres like comedy, horror, mystery, even the western?

LF: When I first started the Machine as a one-man band, I couldn't play it that well. So I dressed in a lot of different costumes, like the Lone Ranger or a soldier. People liked the costumes.

SK: I always feel a little confused when people ask me about genre, and they always do. Because I don't think I'd be good enough at that. I think John Waters does that. For me, I think it gets filtered through this other space as a maker. I actually don't like horror movies. It's something else I like–a morbidity? I don't feel adept enough at camp to pull off genre as an artist.

LF: Stanya, I don't know if you knew about my passion for comedy.

SK: No, I didn't at all. But I could intuit it from your work. When I saw your paintings, they struck me as familiar from a place of pathos and humor; the sad-funny-sad right next to each other, and that's just how I feel. Not humor as in tropes of comedy but a deeper humor. Just the gesture to make a 3-D space in a painting–there's levity to doing that and to breaking the rules of painting. It's funny to break rules, and it didn't seem pretentious. It seemed authentic.

LF: To me, comedy is a part of my life. As a kid I wanted to be a cartoonist and a comedian, so it's always been in me, and obviously it's in you too. And that gets combined with other things like dead animals. I can remember my first interest being in collecting animal skulls. Pairing those two things is not particularly normal. [*Laughter.*]

SK: I'm deeply compelled by the wild world too, and even when it dies. I'm constantly filming it, and for whatever reason, I project onto the wildness of animals and plants. This goes back to our discussion about failure and persistence. Animals are programmed to persist on an impulse level. The impulse to say, "Oh fuck it," and give up on life, that's a human thing. So I'm interested in that persistence. But who else persists? Comedians! That's what comedy is: joking your way through the worst fucking shit in a world full of people going, "Oh fuck it."

LF: Comedians just have to let all this stuff out, and they feel comfortable doing it onstage. And I don't see that as any different from making music. It's a great thing to learn a craft–the way you get information in your mind, and you can just draw it out in any form you want.

SK: It's the same with any making, writing, connecting. These are all ways that people persist. And improvisation is that weird combination of the will to survive and the agility to do so at a moment's notice. It's such an animal thing.

LF: And it's also about being one with something. When I'm on my Machine playing music, everything is happening at once. I can just play and talk and use my whole body and get into it. It took a long time, but like you say, Stanya, if you stick with something, it's going to go somewhere. It's when you give up and you rest on your laurels or just copy yourself again, that's when you're in trouble.

Overleaf:
Stanya Kahn and Llyn Foulkes
Happy Song for You, 2011
(installation view)

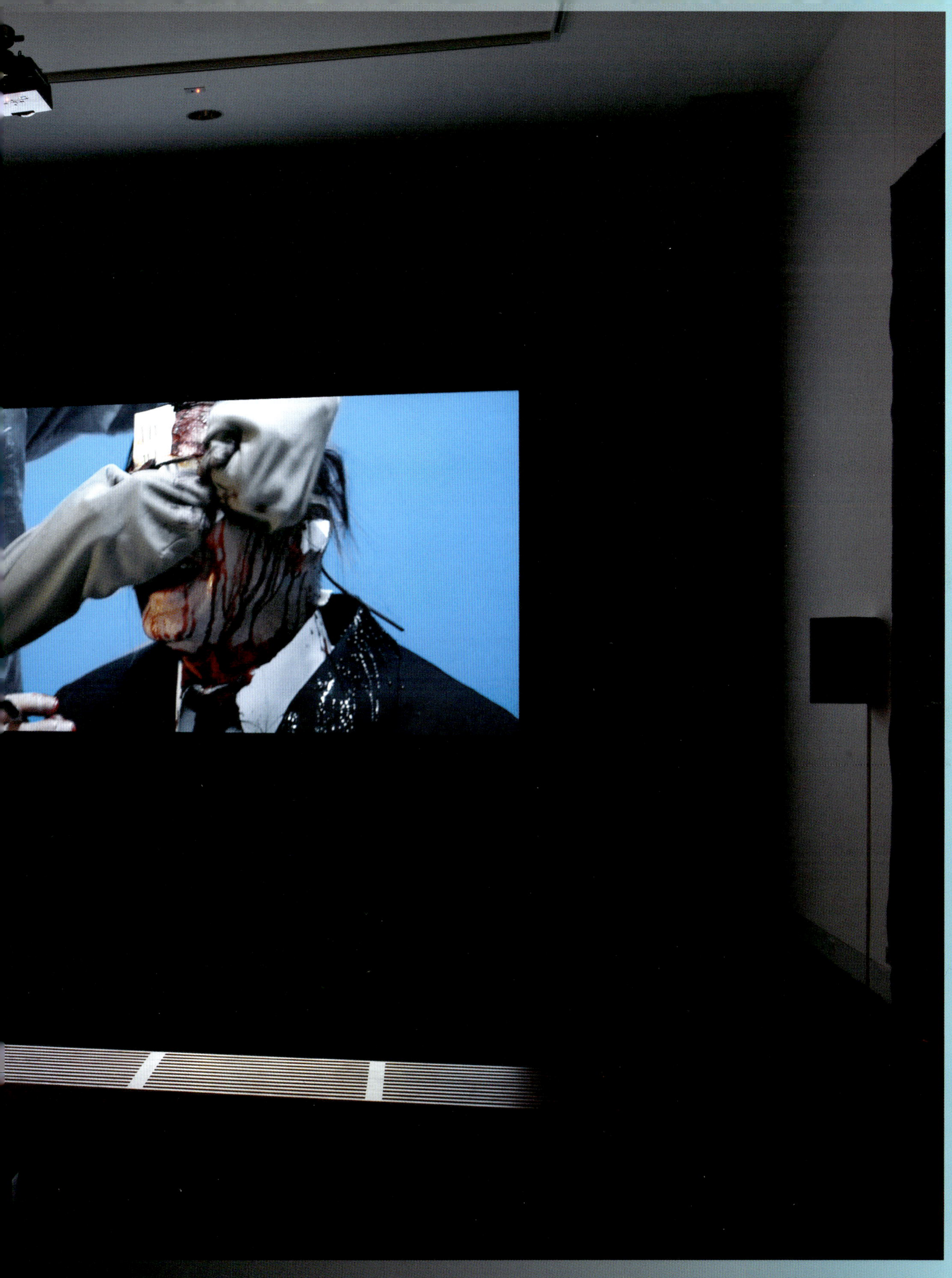

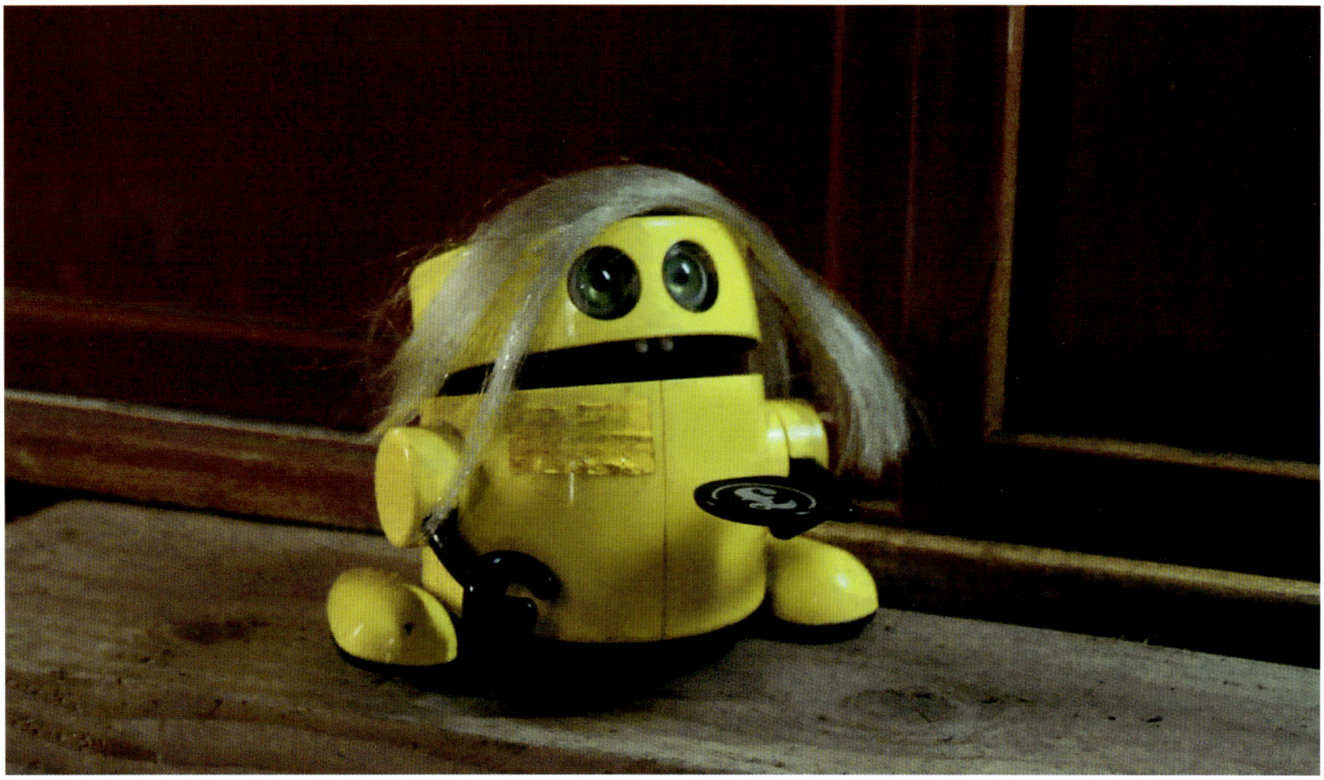

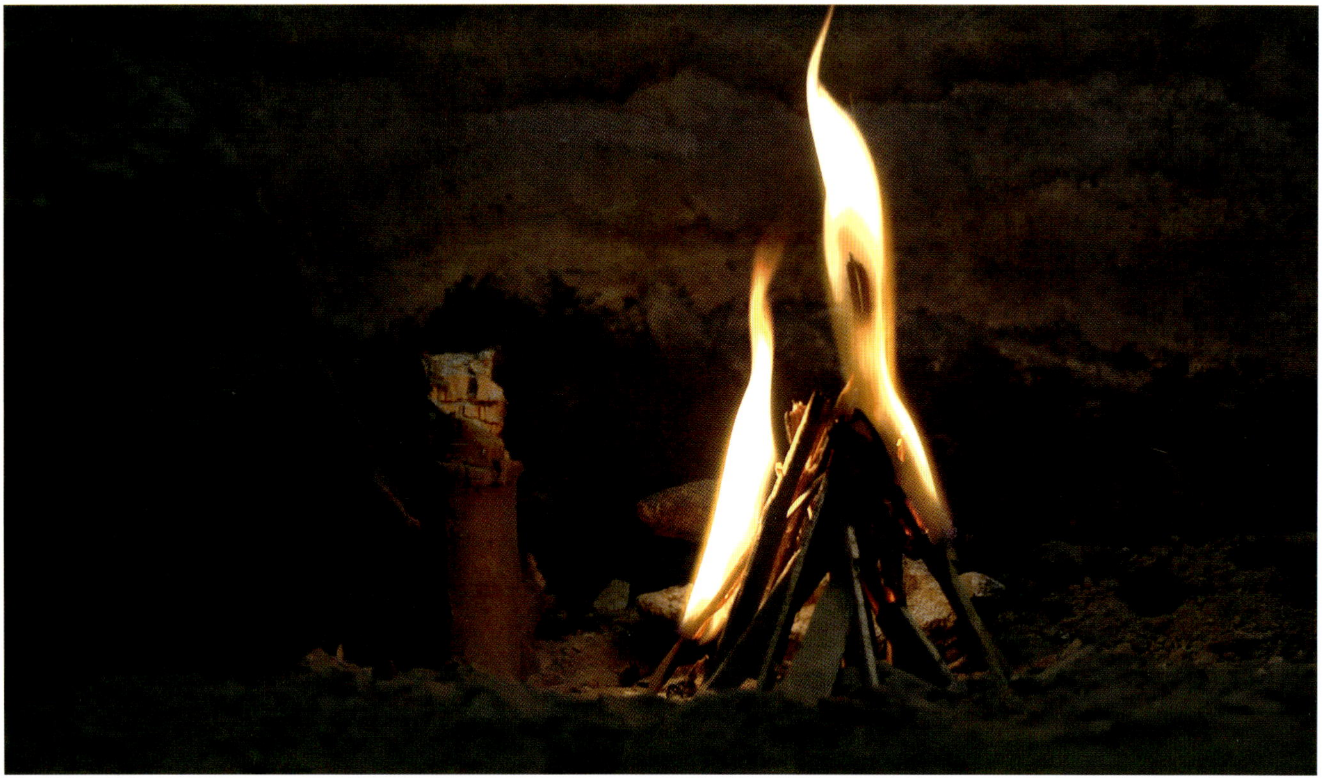

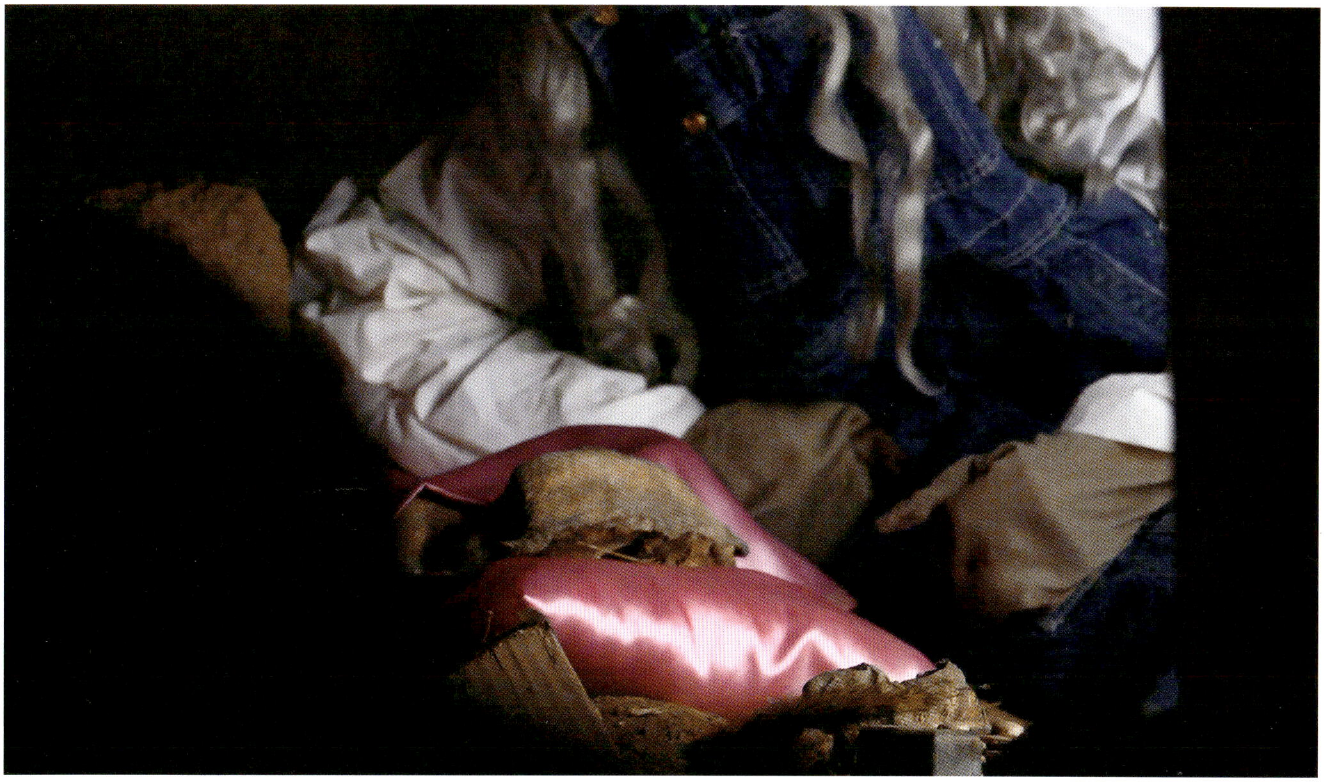

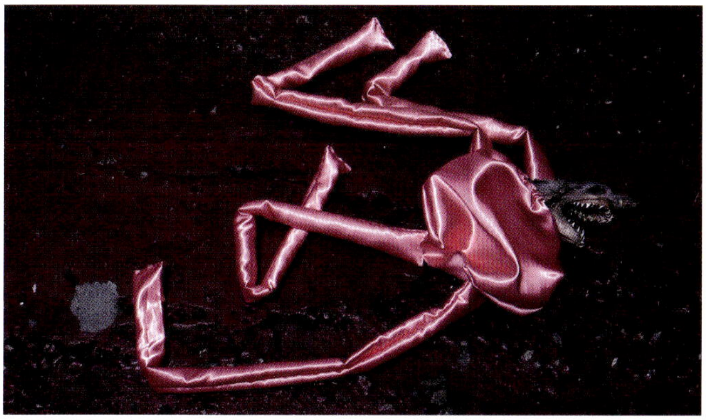

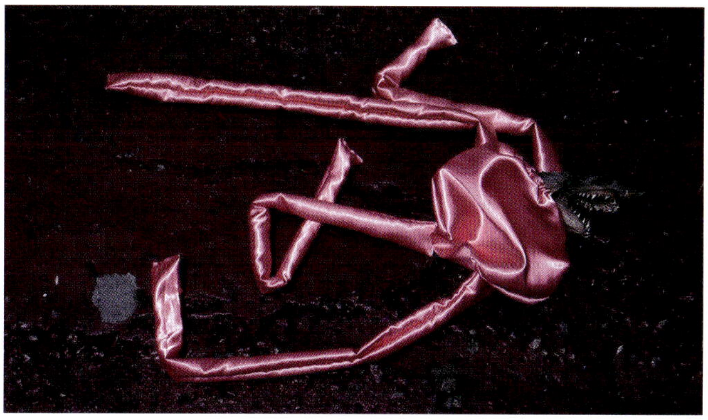

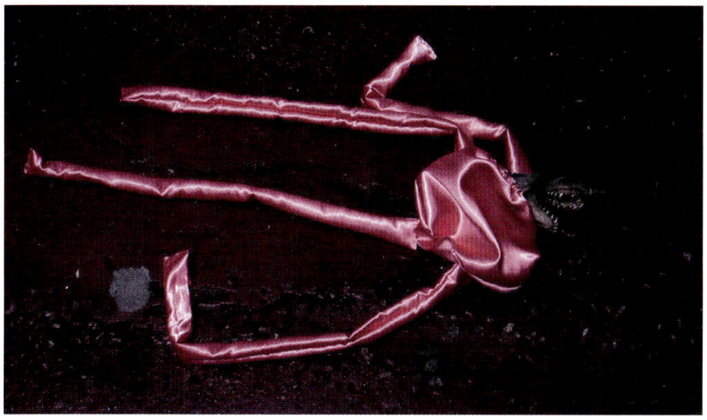

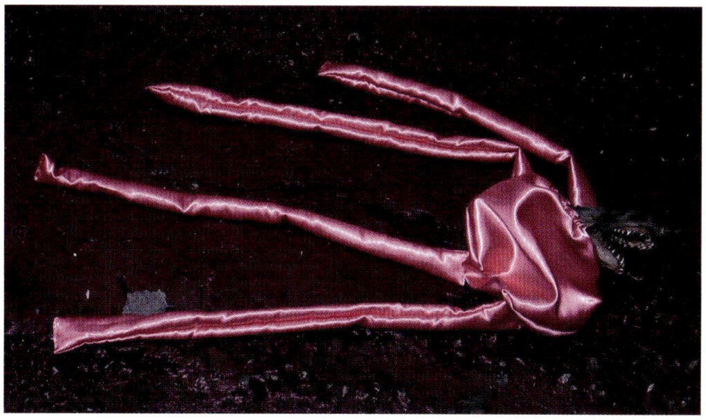

Stanya Kahn and Llyn Foulkes
Stills from *Happy Song for You*, 2011

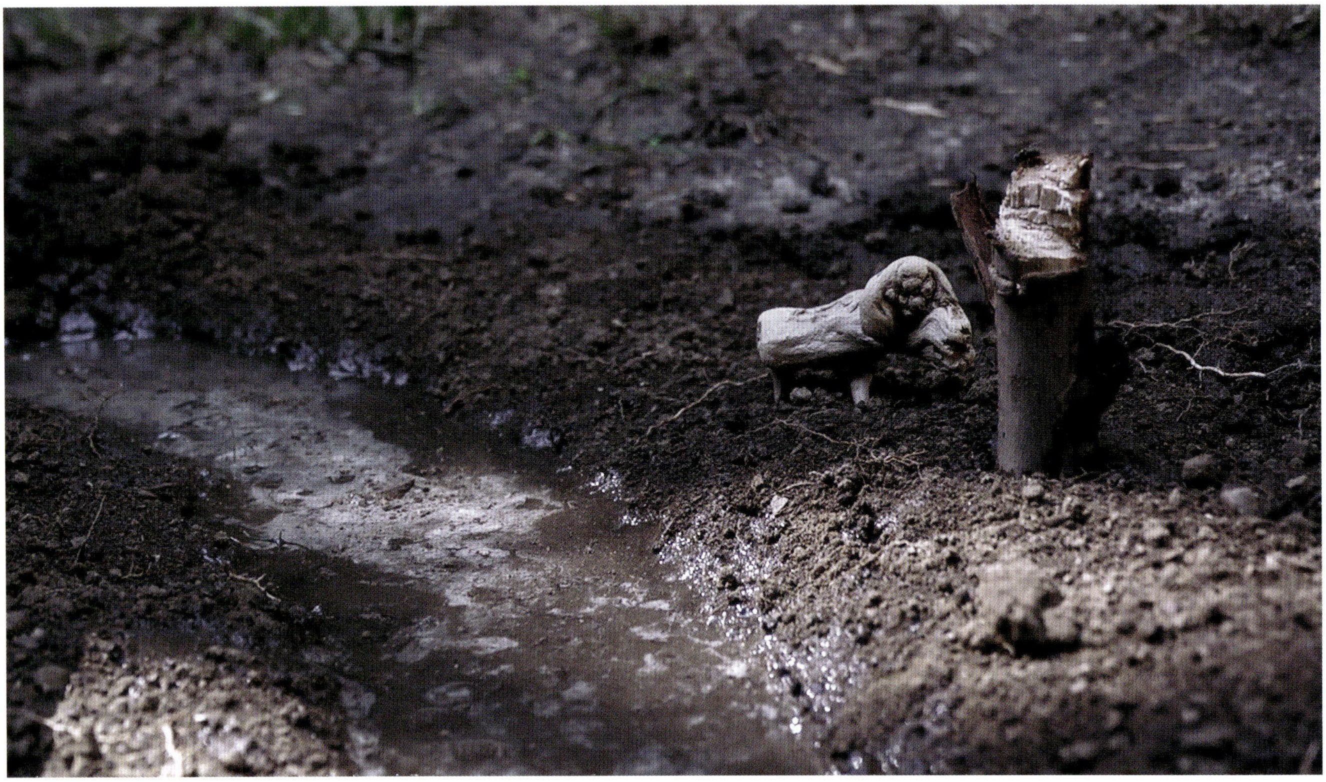

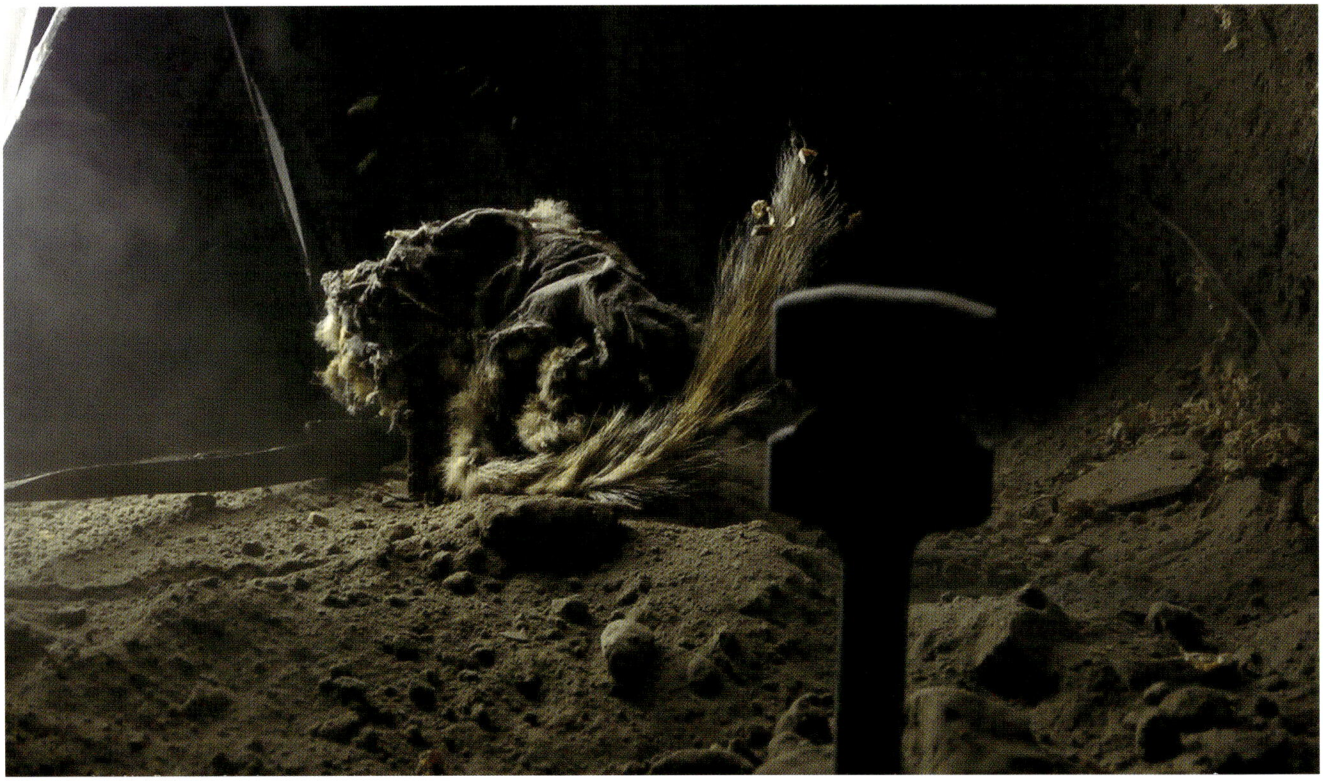

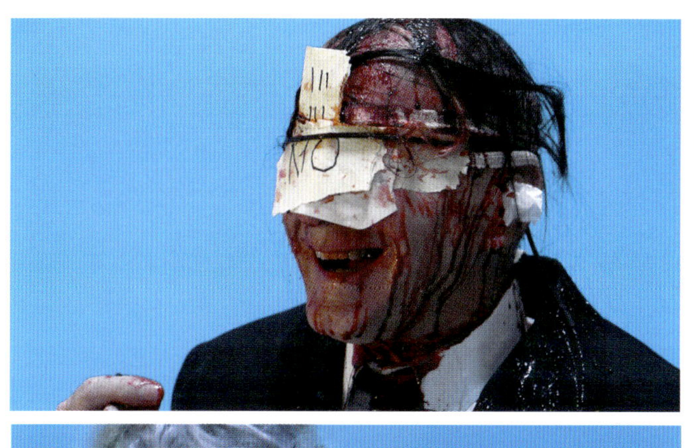
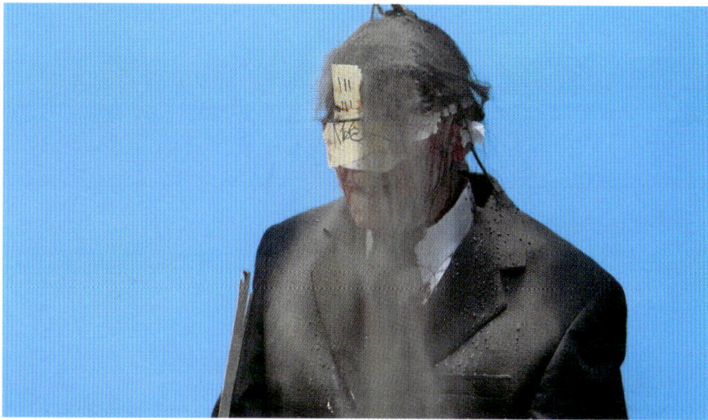
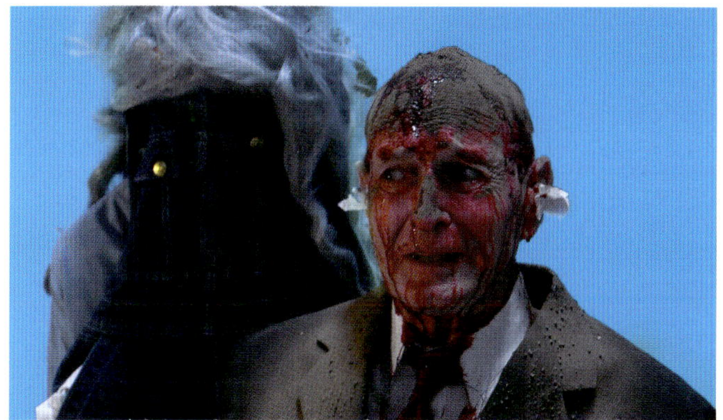
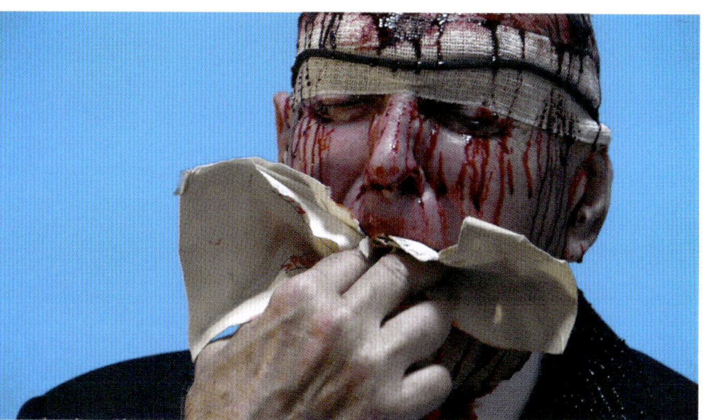

Stanya Kahn and Llyn Foulkes
Stills from *Happy Song for You*, 2011

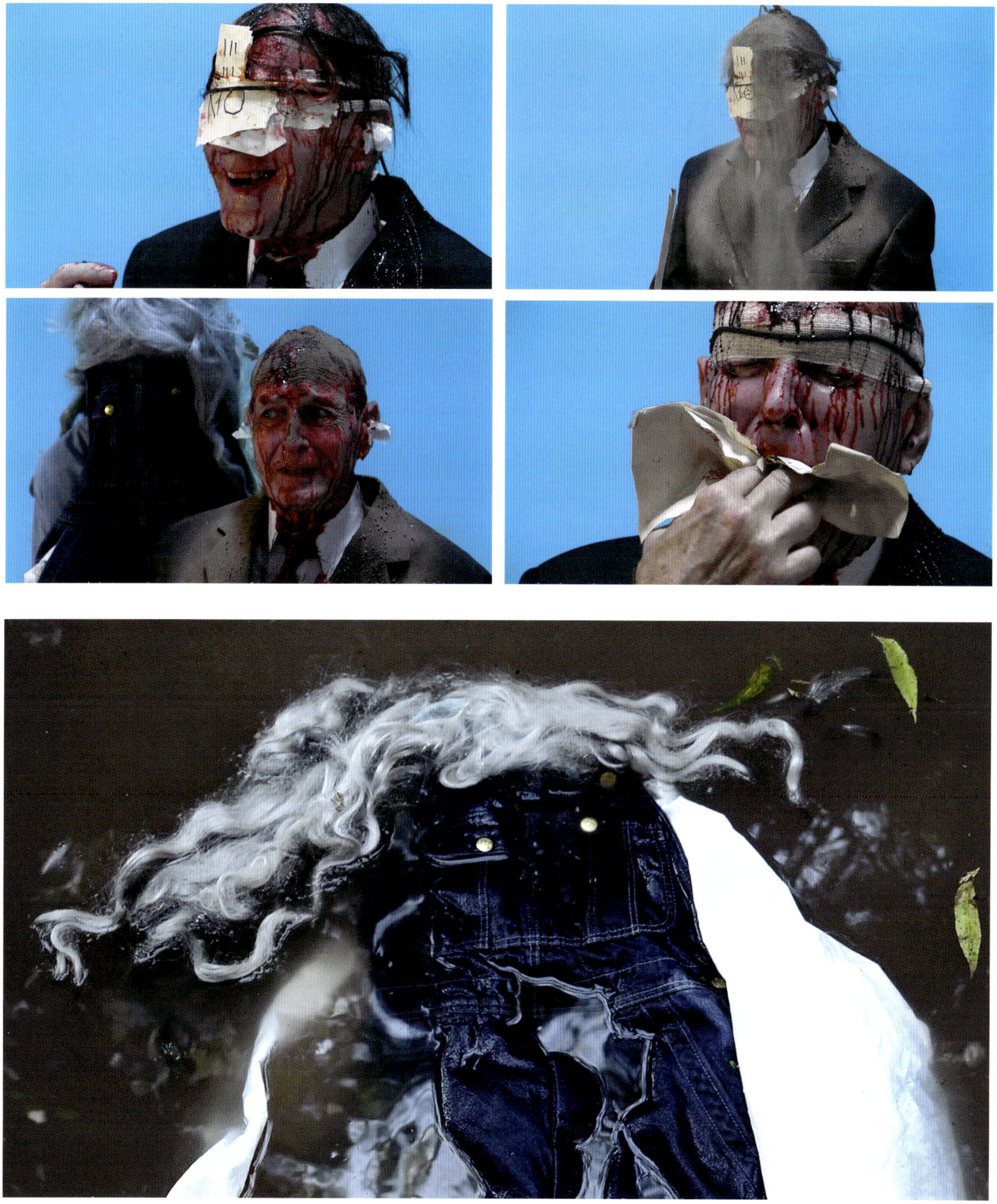

SHANA LUTKER AND JOHN BALDESSARI *A->B*, 2011

A->B is a participatory installation that invites a viewer to select objects from one table and arrange them on another. For Shana Lutker and John Baldessari, the art-making process is rooted in the act of decision making: choice and selection. The structure of *A->B* was developed by the artists from a teaching exercise that Baldessari has implemented in the past. He states: "My motivation for the teaching device was to see what happens when someone moves stuff from one surface to another. Would they replicate the arrangement? Would they sort by size, color, function? Could one sense an underlying principle that they all responded to? There could be all kinds of reasons."

Isolating the impulse to choose and activating the instinct to sort, this installation allows and acknowledges differences in individual choice, mirroring how an artist works in the studio, how a curator selects work for the galleries, or how an art collector chooses acquisitions. The objects were selected by the artists. Items such as a wine bottle and a guitar may reference traditional still-life painting, while domestic and consumer items refer to contemporary material culture. Each participant's arrangement is captured on a live-feed video camera and presented instantaneously on monitors located outside the room installation for public viewing. Lutker's work often investigates personal desire through deconstructing dreams and the unconscious, whereas Baldessari's cultivates opportunities to create works of art through trial and error and chance, and this project uses commonalities between how the artists think about making art. The project combines the personal element of choice with the public act of presenting one's selections.

Shana Lutker and John Baldessari
A -> B, 2011 (installation view)

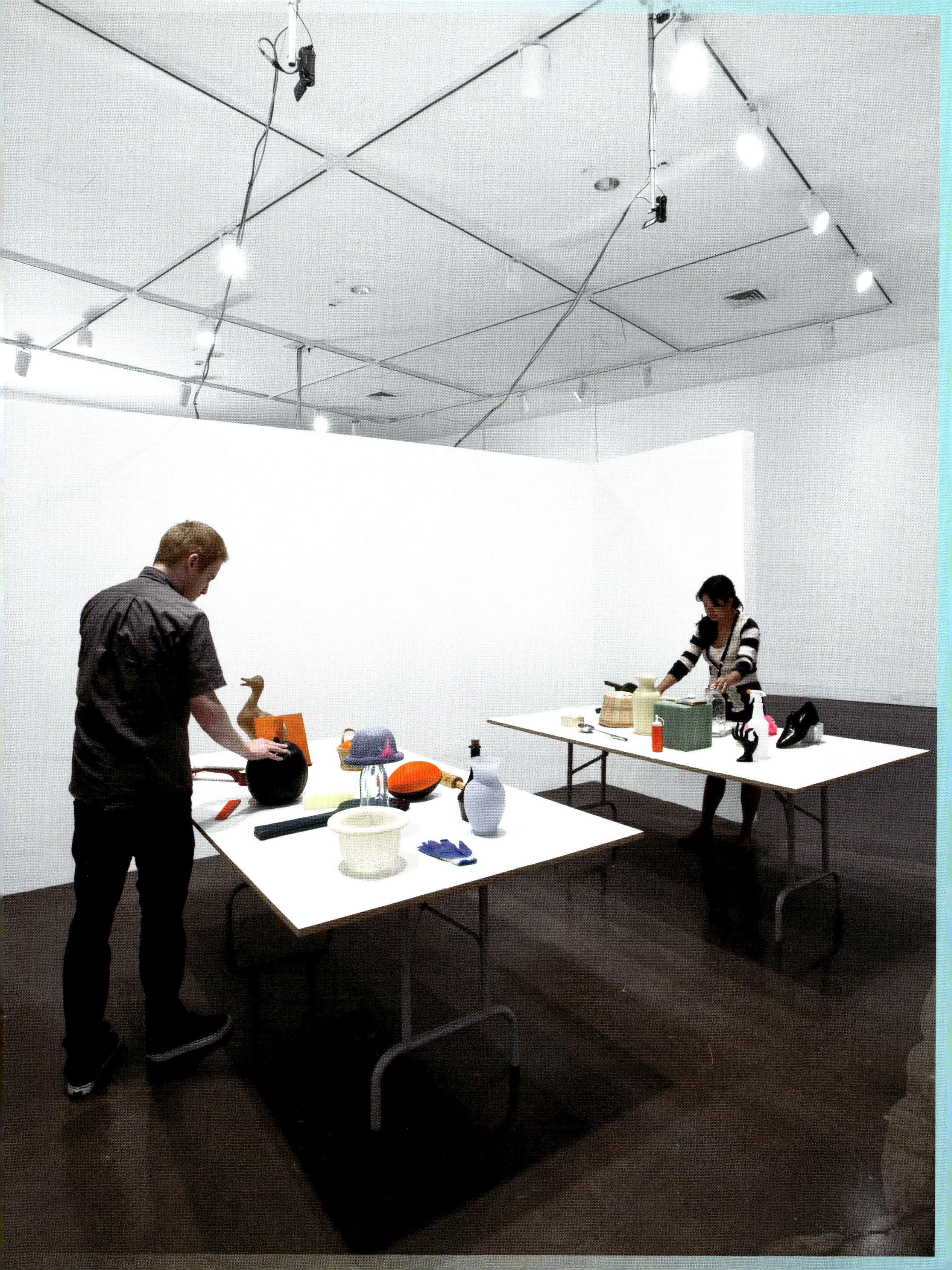

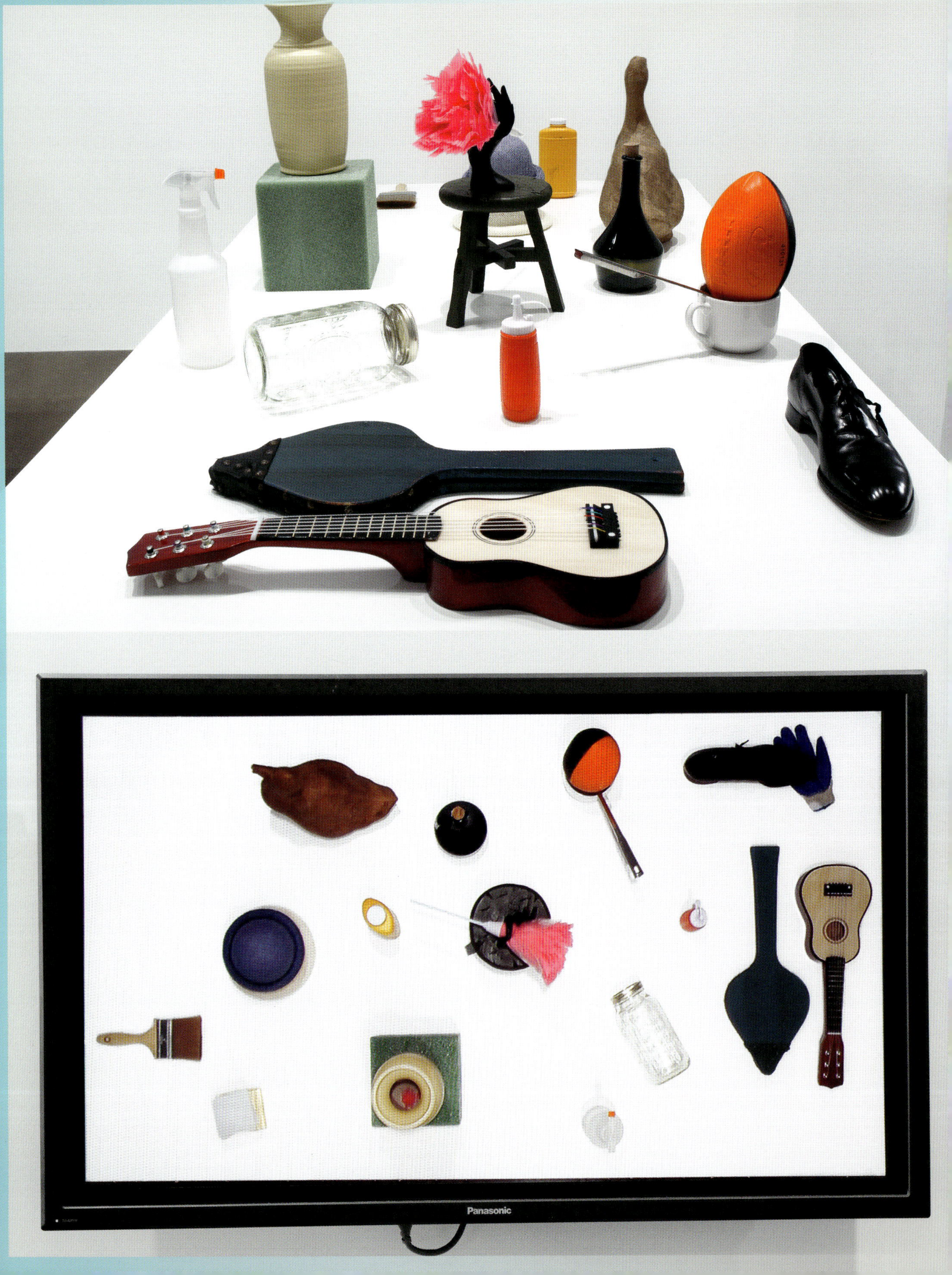

Panasonic

Shana Lutker and John Baldessari

Interview by Constance Lewallen

Shana Lutker and John Baldessari
A -> B, 2011
Top: table and props
Bottom: monitor with live-feed image of tabletop

CL: How did the two of you get matched to do a collaboration?

JB: Sarah Bancroft proposed that I collaborate with Shana, and I immediately said yes. I've done several collaborations with ex-students, and I have always found that I do something I haven't done before.

CL: It doesn't surprise me to hear you say that, since I know that in your many years of teaching you were able to make the experience generative for your own work.

JB: Yes, that's true, and I like the challenge of collaboration.

CL: How did you proceed?

SL: We both knew that we wanted to have focused meetings to quickly outline what would be possible and what would be interesting for both of us to pursue.

JB: It doesn't always work, though. If it's truly collaboration, it's not the work of two people but a symbiosis.

CL: What William Burroughs and Brion Gysin called "the third mind."

JB: Yeah, yeah.

CL: Do you feel that you have things in common in your respective work?

SL: Yes. Before meeting with John, I made a list of concerns that we shared in our work. One was decision making; making choices is, in many ways, what making art is. It's what everything is, but artists isolate the act of decision.

JB: For me it's perfect, fundamental to the way I work.

CL: An interest in language is another point of commonality between the two of you.

SL: That was on my list too.

CL: How about humor and the absurd?

SL: Yes, for sure.

CL: In my estimation, a lot of work by younger artists is rooted in the work of John's generation.

JB: That's been said many times, but why?

CL: Because in the late sixties and early seventies artists were inventing new forms, breaking new ground, doing things that hadn't been done. It was a time of change, not only artistically but also in the world at large—a time of major change. The artists of that time created a vocabulary that is still current. For example, the then new forms of photo and text, video, and performance are taken for granted today.

JB: Right.

SL: Looking back, I tend to skip the previous decade or two and turn instead to the era of my parents.

JB: Would you call it nostalgia?

SL: I was born in 1978, so the sixties and seventies were not a part of my life, but those decades are still so important in determining the culture and politics today.... So, yes, I have nostalgia for a time I never actually knew.

JB: There was a time when everyone thought the world might change.

CL: We thought so, and we were wrong. [*Laughter.*]

SL: Now we can see that, but you can't see it with the same distance as I can because you lived it.

CL: Sad but true.

SL: But it can be productive to know what happened, to evaluate what actually was possible or not possible, to be able to see where the momentum is now and predict where it will go.

JB: What about the antimateriality argument?

SL: The idea that making objects is not important?

JB: Or that art was too much about making money.

SL: In the sixties or seventies non-object art was conceived in rebellion against painting and the money and attention that came to New York and the abstract expressionists in the fifties. A return to object making characterized the eighties. During the nineties—well, who knows what happened!

CL: In the nineties artists began to look back to the sixties and seventies, but that was also the era of relational aesthetics, of art being about sharing and giving, but even that wasn't entirely new.

SL: There was a lot of idealism around relational aesthetics, but it was like a balloon that was overinflated and then popped. Interactive work wasn't new to the nineties. And now, when an artist makes an interactive work, it doesn't necessarily fall under the rubric of relational aesthetics. And there's a new pessimism around that kind of work.

JB: It was like feeding the homeless was brought into an art gallery. Back then we just called it feeding the homeless, not relational aesthetics.

CL: Shana, you have made sculptural objects, such as a crutch and a bottle holder, that were derived from your dreams.

JB: I like that work a lot.

CL: Those objects have been described as uncanny.

SL: I was rereading Freud on the uncanny yesterday. He describes how dismembered limbs, pieces of the body, are essentially a definition of uncanny, which made me think of John's pieces, the noses and ears. You work with images, John, to produce uncanny moments, but they are always rooted in a source—they come from something. I work similarly. My objects come from something, from text or from photographic images. The uncanny is in between real space and unconscious space.

JB: "In between" is an idea that I like a lot. We both work in that in-between space but in different ways.

CL: Getting back to your collaboration, what are you planning to do?

SL: We want to be true to the nature of collaboration. Never did we talk about making pieces individually and exhibiting them together. Instead we discussed how we could make a work or a structure. We decided to set up a situation that can be changed by the viewer. We are collaborating with the museum public, the museum itself.

CL: So it's an interactive piece.

JB: We are creating a situation where art might happen. It's almost like teaching.

SL: In our first meeting, John mentioned a teaching exercise he did at CalArts. He would put a group of objects on a table and send one person into the room to arrange the objects on a second table while others waited outside. Then everyone would go in and see how the student had arranged the objects. That was the starting point for our piece. I find it interesting because it involves decision making. It is a mirror for how an artist works in the studio. It also allows and acknowledges the differences in individual choice.

JB: We should describe what we are going to do. [*Laughter.*]

SL: There will be two tables, and on one there will be a lot of things.

CL: Ordinary things?

JB: Stuff. My motivation for the teaching device was to see what happens when someone moves stuff from one surface to another. Would they replicate the arrangement? Probably not. Would they sort by size, color, function? Would there be a through line among all the students? Could one sense an underlying principle that they all responded to? There could be all kinds of reasons.

CL: So in the gallery there will be objects on one table for people to move to the other table.

JB: If they want to. We don't know if they will. There will be an overhead camera so viewers will see two tables projected large on the wall of the gallery, and if anyone is participating, you can see that happening.

SL: The tables will be behind the wall onto which the image is projected.

CL: Will there be a sign that clues in visitors?

JB: Yes. Before the exhibition opens, we might invite trustees or staff or kids, who are great at this stuff, to participate. We could photograph some of their activity to give visitors to the show the idea. I always keep in my mind what George Bernard Shaw said, something like, "Labor is always divided into two parts." In moving material from point A to point B, there will be people who direct and people who do it.

SL: We hope that when people see a projection of what's going on behind the wall they will realize that they can go inside. There will be an "aha!" moment as the viewer understands the structure of the piece.

JB: We worry that there may not be enough bait or intrigue for people to want to participate. Or that it will be embarrassing. I have biases like that. I don't want to be a part of someone else's artwork.

CL: Once your collaboration is up and running, will the activity be recorded?

JB: Ideally it would, but there are budgetary restraints. We had to pare down the idea to bare bones.

SL: We considered taking photographs of the arrangements at intervals.

JB: I did that at LACMA once. Museum visitors could rearrange objects from a still life, and each time there was a printout that was posted. At the end of the show there were hundreds. They could also take theirs home as a souvenir.

CL: I curated a show recently that allowed for viewer participation but found that not many engaged in the work.

JB: Most spectators want to be passive.

CL: Shana, you work in many media—sculpture, text, photography—which is something John has always done too. It was important to artists of John's generation not to be tied to a medium. Now no one even thinks about it.

JB: One phrase you hear a lot recently is "sculpting in time," which refers to nonstatic forms, like performance and film.

CL: Shana, it seems like you are drawn to surrealism.

SL: Yes, I like the way surrealists consider reason, desire, and chance, and how that affects our relationship to the others and to objects.

JB: Our project is right out of surrealism—dissecting tables.

CL: Are you going to choose objects according to any particular plan?

JB: We haven't gotten that far. But a lot of this thinking comes out of traditional art classes. Most schools have a closet they call the still-life room with miscellaneous objects. Basically that's what this is about. We might want to go to one of the local colleges and borrow their stuff. What's in the closet is interesting too. Usually it's going to be wine bottles, a cow's skull, a guitar, classical sculpture. [*Laughter.*] That would lean it in one direction. Or we could just pick up things from Goodwill.

CL: Well, the first plan will hark back to art history—early twentieth-century still life—and the latter will refer to contemporary material culture.

JB: We could go either way. We discussed how, when collections are donated to Goodwill, people have to sort them.

SL: They sort all the plates, vases, clothing and then assign prices by type. For my own work, I have been buying or finding objects that seem particular or special in some way, which show their history, but John and I have been talking about generic, impersonal objects.

JB: It really doesn't matter.

CL: Shana, I read that you collected all the *New York Times* newspapers from certain years.

SL: Yes, I have all the *Times* from 2003 to 2008, though I have been thinking about throwing them away.

JB: We both have a hard time throwing things away.

SL: I started the collection when I moved to Los Angeles. Receiving the *New York Times*, even though it was printed here in Los Angeles, was about maintaining this connection to New York. During that time the newspapers began to be archived digitally, without the ads, so I took it upon myself to save the ads and layouts. There must be other archives of physical newspapers, but most libraries don't have them anymore. I made a book of all the subjective viewpoint full-page ads from 2004. I like to read them as an alternative to the news reports.

CL: Did I read that you call the studio a place of anxiety?

SL: That sounds like something I would say.

CL: I guess that's true of anyone's workplace.

SL: But making art is different from being a lawyer or doctor, perhaps because in those professions there is always some other authority that can tell you what's right or wrong. In art there isn't that.

JB: No job description.

SL: That's a good line—and you can't be fired.

CL: You can be discouraged. [*Laughter.*] Shana, how do you feel about living in Los Angeles? You could have moved back to New York after you graduated.

SL: I think about moving back almost every day. [*Laughter.*] But I stay in Los Angeles because of the community of artists and because it's a place to work; New York is a place to be.

JB: That's essential. Because of the geography of Los Angeles, it's hard to socialize here but too easy in New York. There are too many things going on.

SL: Too many good restaurants and too much art. I think artists need to be familiar with New York. I remain connected to New York through friends, family, and work. You don't have to live there, though.

JB: Peter Plagens was interviewing an eighties painter and asked him why he lived in New York. He replied that it was because of the theater, the movies, the art. Plagens observed that the artist never participated in any of those things, to which the artist replied, "But it's important to know they're there." [*Laughter.*]

CL: There is a lot happening in Los Angeles, but it's so diffuse.

JB: You have to always calculate the time to get where you are going. Do you know Dave Hickey's line, "In Los Angeles, if you look at a show in a gallery for the same amount of time it took you to drive there, it's probably a good show"?

CL: This seems like a good place to end. Thank you both.

Shana Lutker and John Baldessari
A –> B, 2011 (installation view of monitors with live-feed images of tabletops)

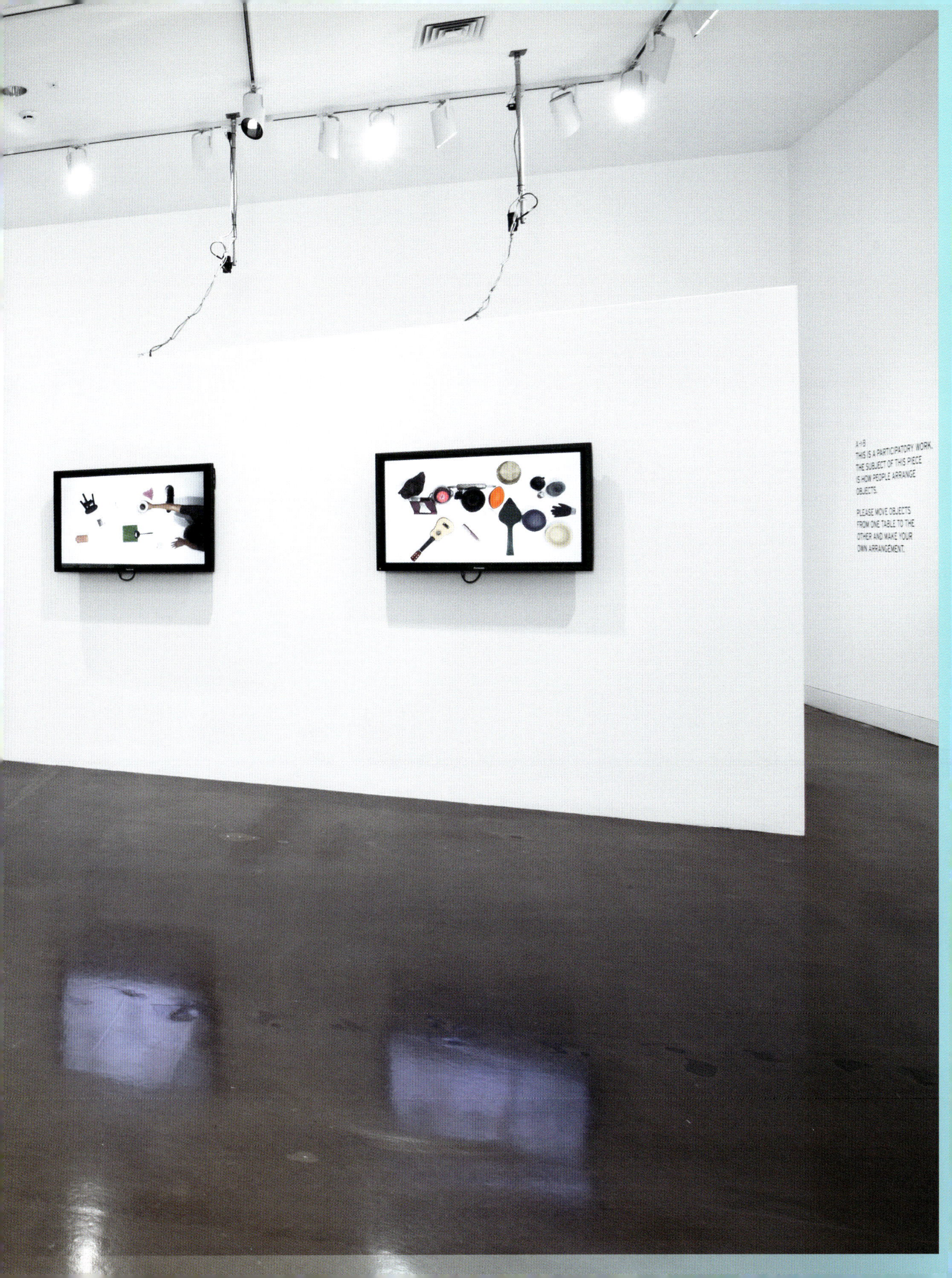
A→B
THIS IS A PARTICIPATORY WORK.
THE SUBJECT OF THIS PIECE
IS HOW PEOPLE ARRANGE
OBJECTS.
PLEASE MOVE OBJECTS
FROM ONE TABLE TO THE
OTHER AND MAKE YOUR
OWN ARRANGEMENT.

A→B

THIS IS A PARTICIPATORY WORK. THE SUBJECT OF THIS PIECE IS HOW PEOPLE ARRANGE OBJECTS.

PLEASE MOVE OBJECTS FROM ONE TABLE TO THE OTHER AND MAKE YOUR OWN ARRANGEMENT.

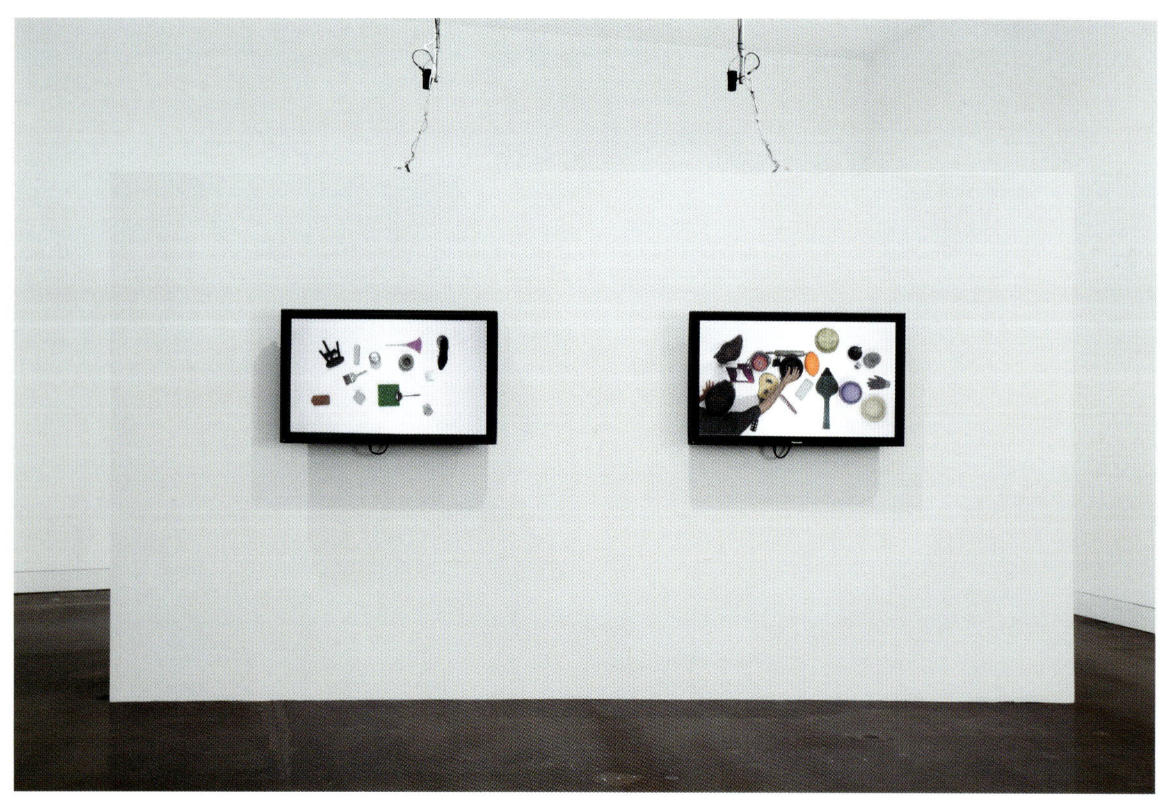

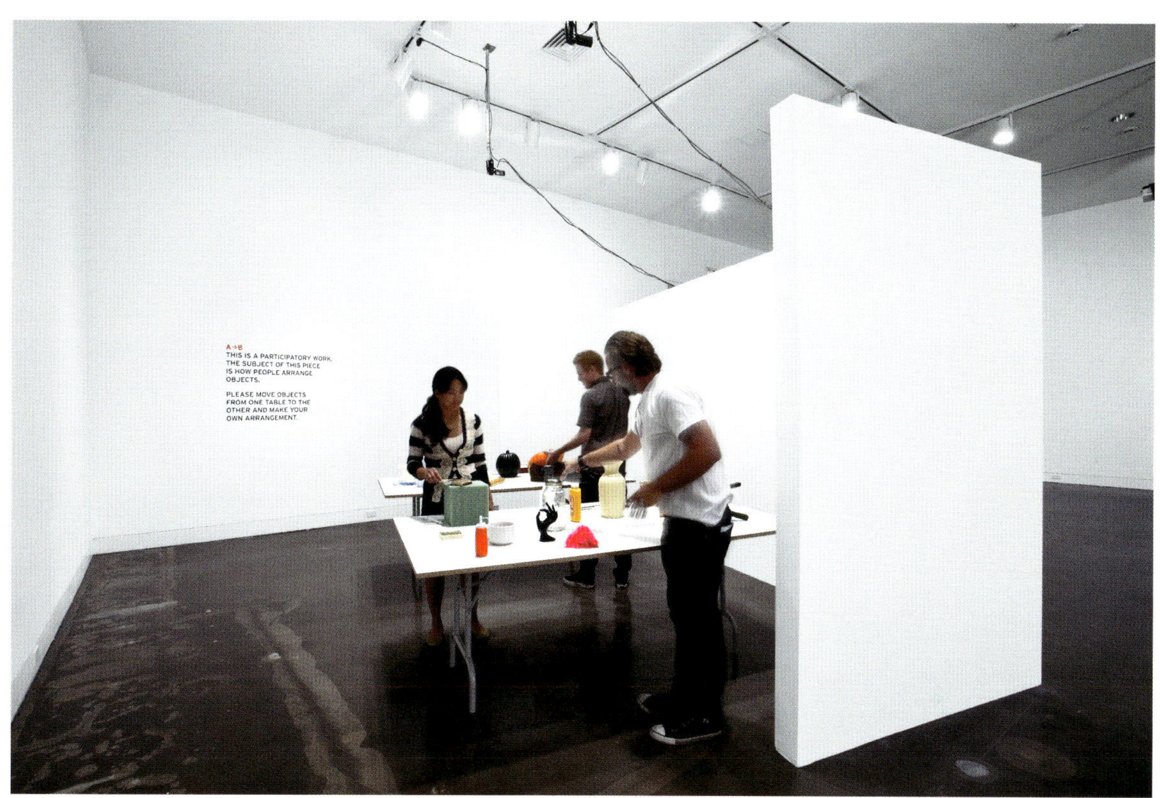

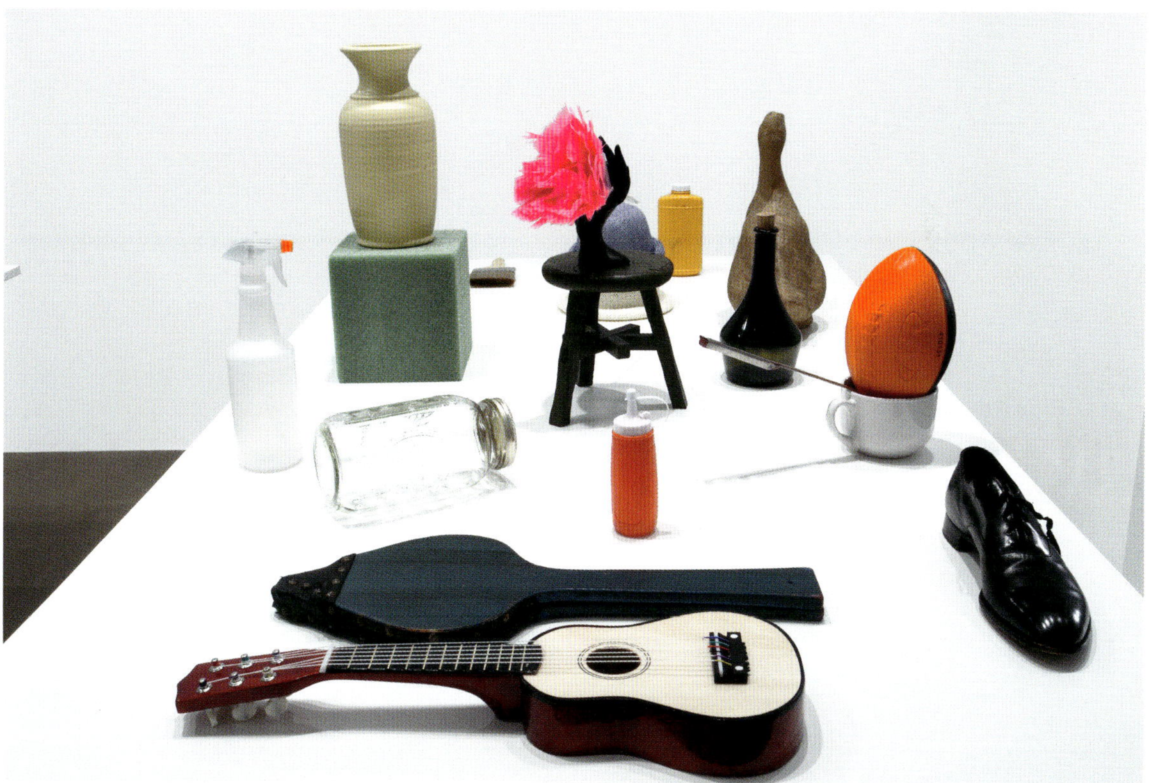

Shana Lutker and John Baldessari
A –> B, 2011 (details and installation views)

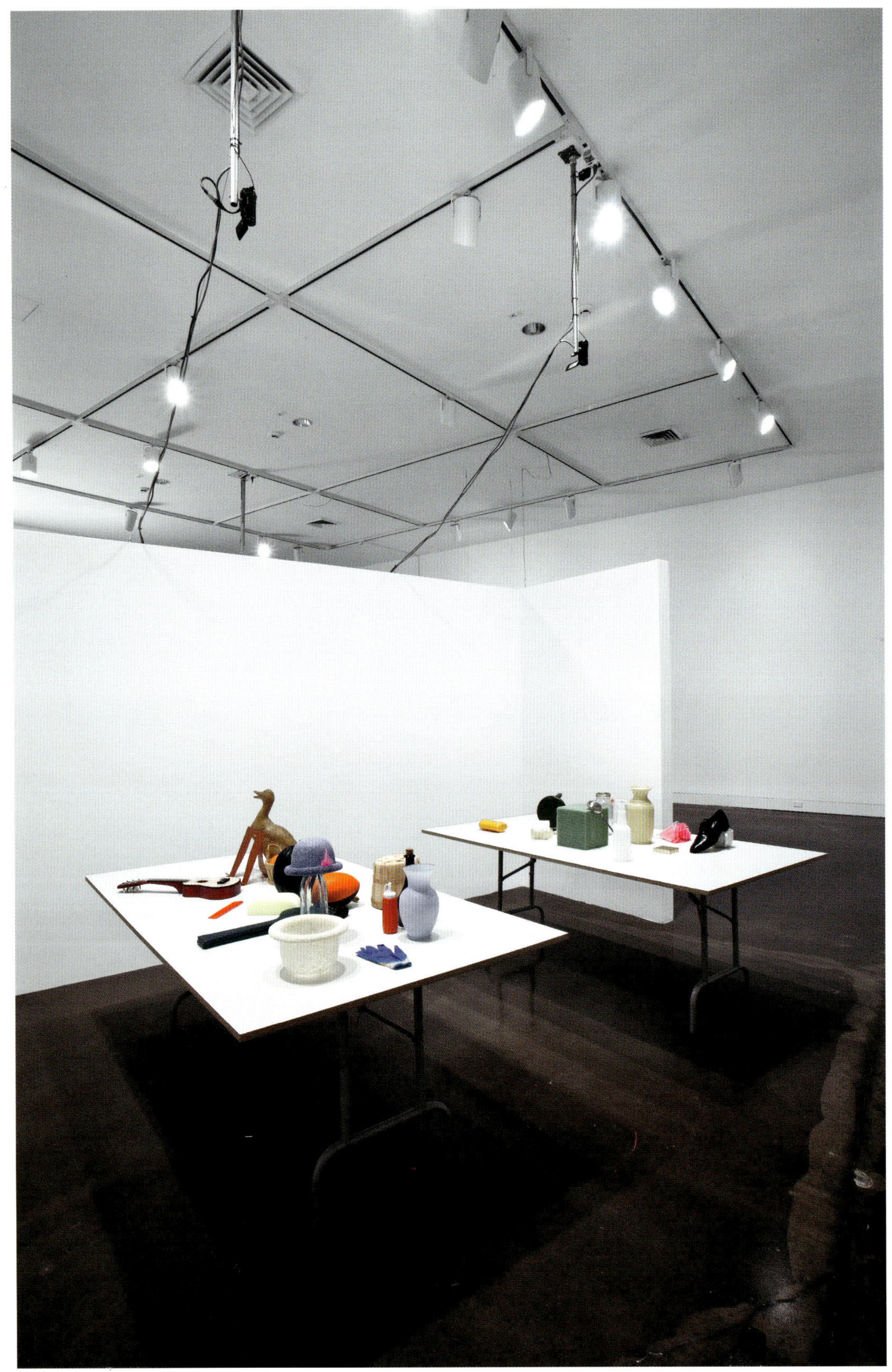

Shana Lutker and John Baldessari
A -> B, 2011 (installation views)

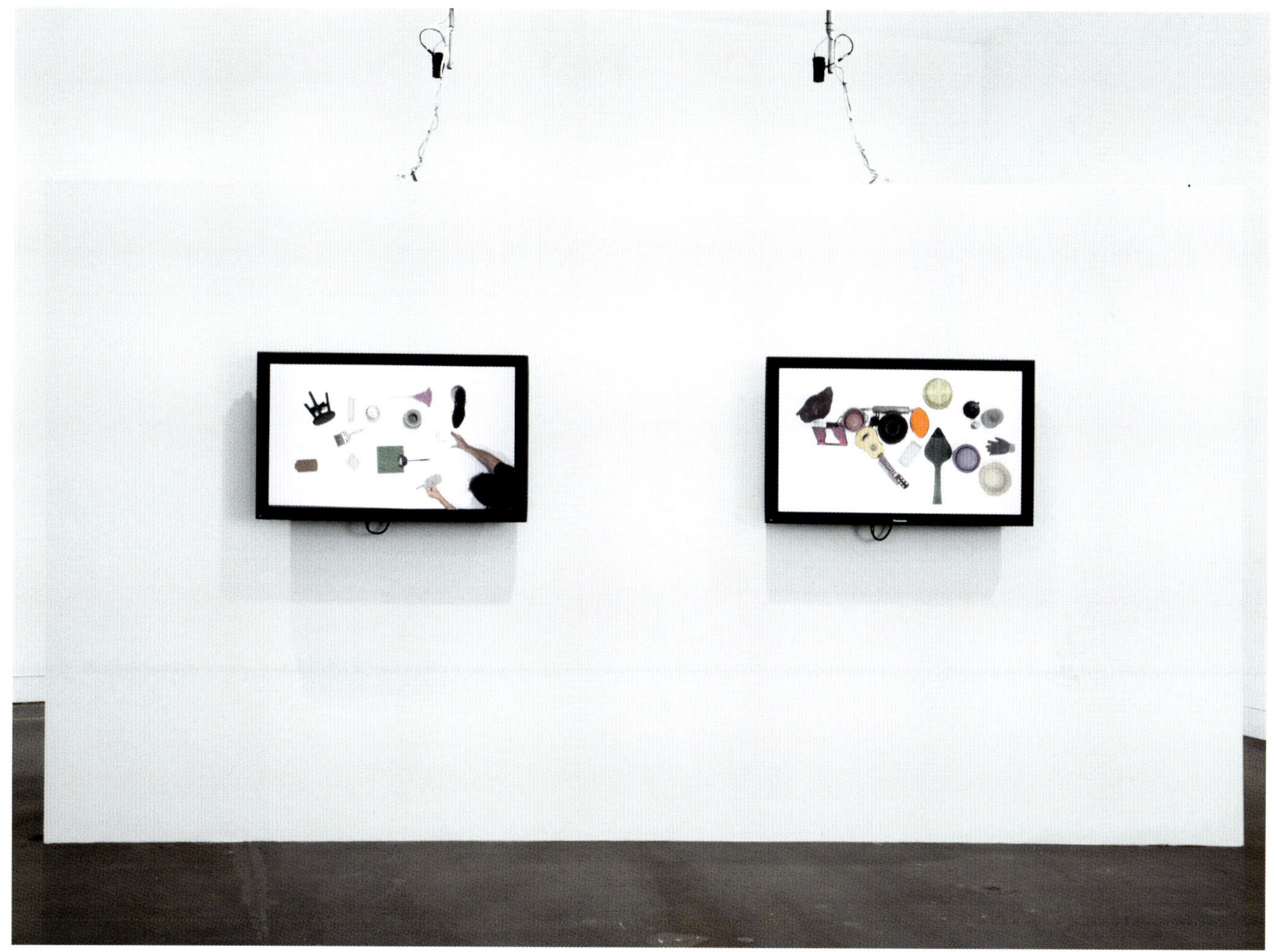

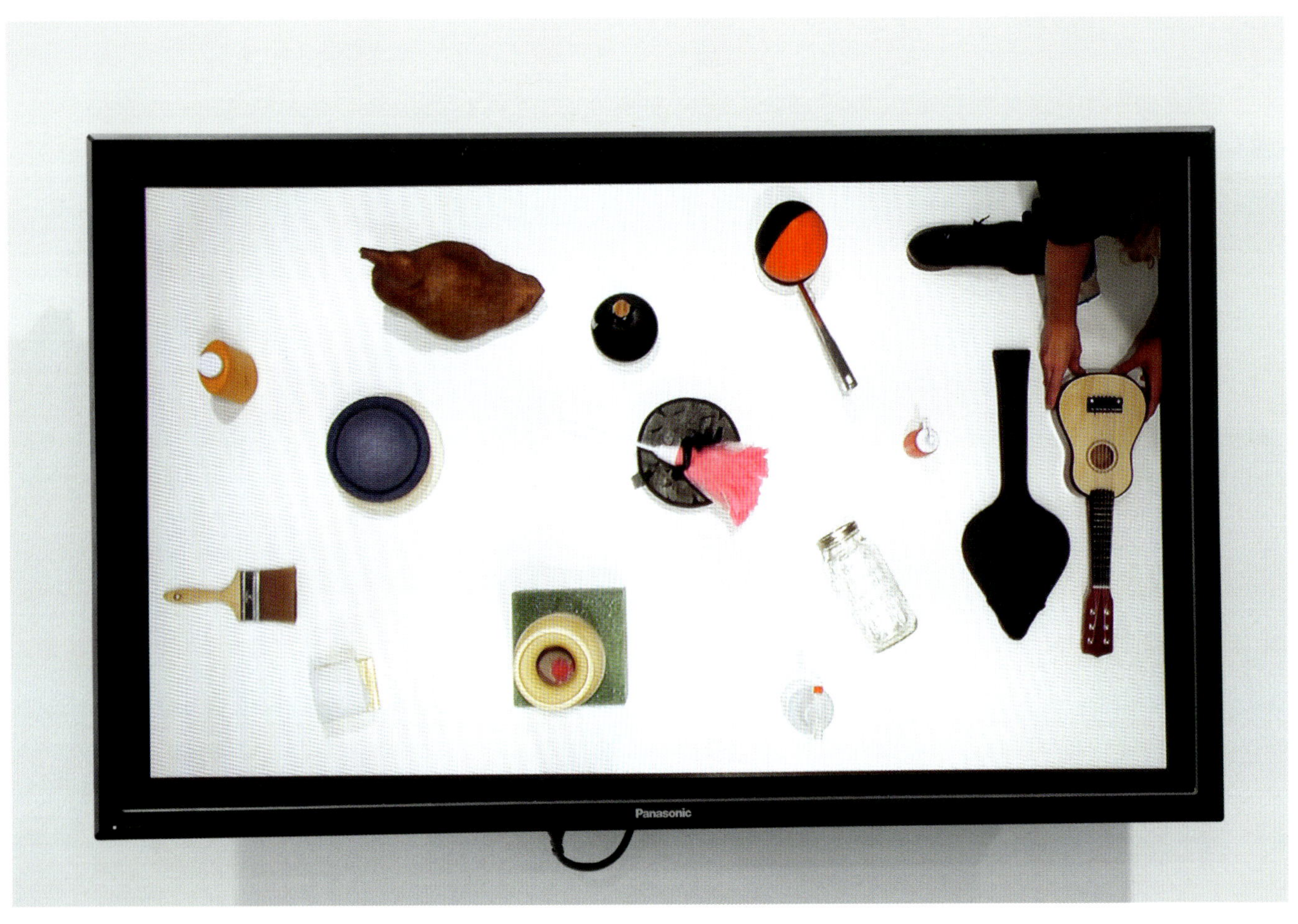
Panasonic

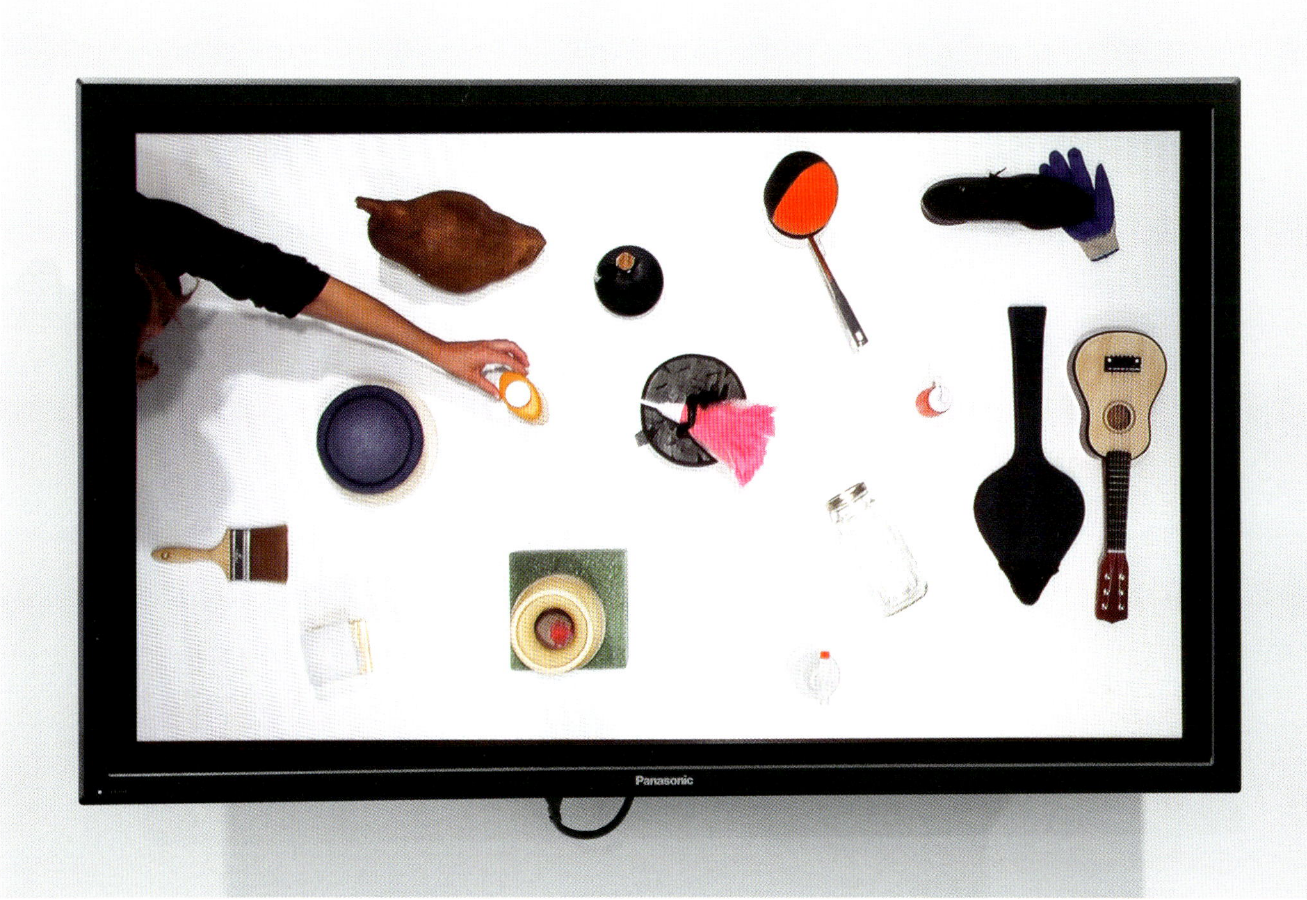

Shana Lutker and John Baldessari
A –> B, 2011 (monitor with live-feed image of tabletop)

AMANDA ROSS-HO AND ALLEN RUPPERSBERG *THE MEANING OF PLUS AND MINUS*, 2011

Amanda Ross-Ho and Allen Ruppersberg's sculptural installation embraces the artists' parallel interests in negotiating the archive through three-dimensional presentations–both artists reference preexisting cultural imagery or objects in their respective practices. The title *The Meaning of Plus and Minus* is borrowed from an educational film in Ruppersberg's collection that teaches the basic arithmetic concepts of addition and subtraction. Ross-Ho and Ruppersberg explain the title: "It suggests positive and negative space, adding and subtracting, and describes what we are physically trying to do. It also refers to past and present, relationships." The installation is a physical manifestation of the artists' collage strategies, featuring a random slide show of images from Ross-Ho's massive photographic archive as well as a continuously looping video of records playing (from Ruppersberg's own collection of 78s), which serves as a sound track for the project. These images are projected onto a large binder fabricated especially for this purpose.

The binder references the ubiquitous role of the book in Ruppersberg's practice as well as the binder's practical use as an organizational device for ephemera in his studio. Fabricated in collaboration with a workshop that specializes in Hollywood props, the binder evolves from a series of sculptural gestures by Ross-Ho in which familiar objects are enlarged with a level of critical detail that creates heightened intimacy with their form and conceptual implications. In its concrete objecthood, the binder acts as a fixed screen for the fluctuation of sound and imagery, suggesting the scale and perpetuity of a never-ending flow of information–a condition critical to the practices of both artists.

Amanda Ross-Ho and Allen Ruppersberg
The Meaning of Plus and Minus, 2011
(installation view)

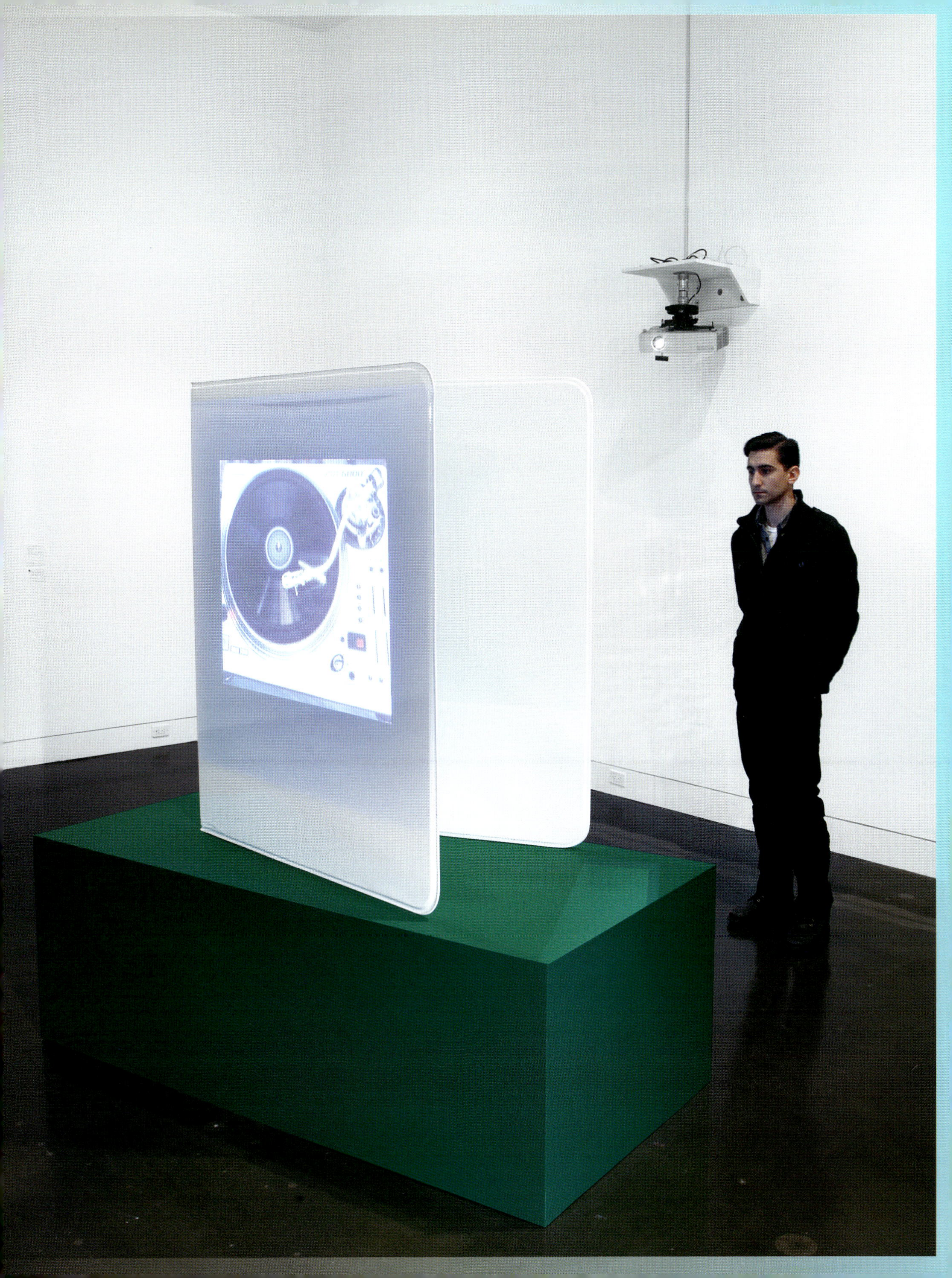

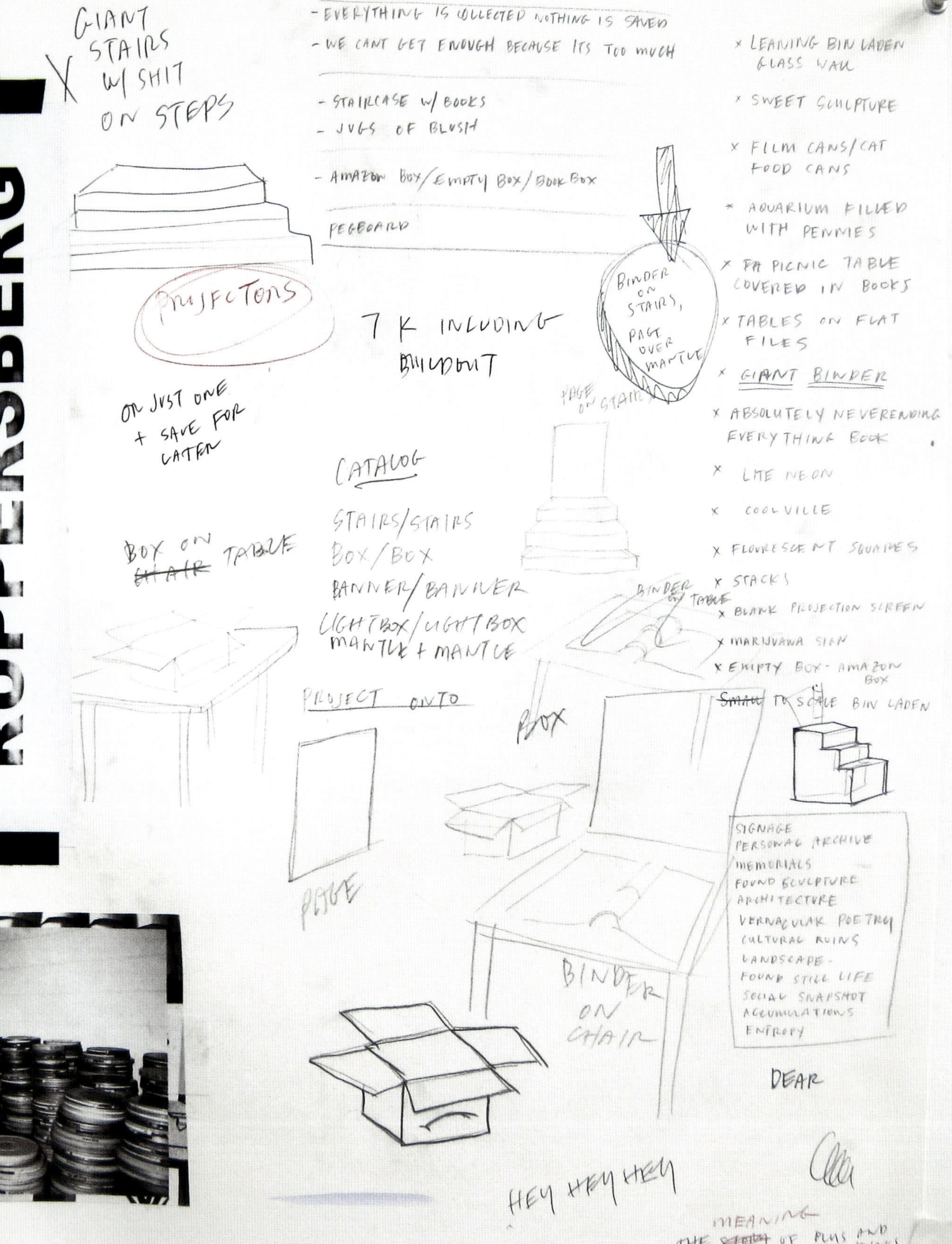

RUPPERSBERG
GIANT STAIRS W/ SHIT ON STEPS
- EVERYTHING IS COLLECTED NOTHING IS SAVED
- WE CANT GET ENOUGH BECAUSE ITS TOO MUCH
- STAIRCASE W/ BOOKS
- JUGS OF BLUSH
- AMAZON BOX/EMPTY BOX/BOOK BOX
PEGBOARD
PROJECTORS
7 K INCLUDING BUILDOUT
ON JUST ONE + SAVE FOR LATER
BINDER ON STAIRS, PAGE OVER MANTLE
PAGE ON STAIRS
× LEANING BIN LADEN GLASS WALL
× SWEET SCULPTURE
× FILM CANS/CAT FOOD CANS
× AQUARIUM FILLED WITH PENNIES
× PICNIC TABLE COVERED IN BOOKS
× TABLES ON FLAT FILES
× GIANT BINDER
× ABSOLUTELY NEVERENDING EVERYTHING BOOK
× LITE NEON
× COOLVILLE
× FLOURESCENT SQUARES
× STACKS
× BLANK PROJECTION SCREEN
× MARIJUANA SIGN
× EMPTY BOX - AMAZON BOX
TO SCALE BIN LADEN
CATALOG
STAIRS/STAIRS
BOX/BOX
BANNER/BANNER
LIGHTBOX/LIGHTBOX
MANTLE + MANTLE
BOX ON TABLE
BINDER ON TABLE
PROJECT ONTO
BOX
PAGE
BINDER ON CHAIR
SIGNAGE
PERSONAL ARCHIVE
MEMORIALS
FOUND SCULPTURE
ARCHITECTURE
VERNACULAR POETRY
CULTURAL RUINS
LANDSCAPE
FOUND STILL LIFE
SOCIAL SNAPSHOT
ACCUMULATIONS
ENTROPY
DEAR
HEY HEY HEY
THE MEANING OF PLUS AND MINUS

Amanda Ross-Ho and Allen Ruppersberg

Interview by Constance Lewallen

Amanda Ross-Ho
Working drawing for *The Meaning of Plus and Minus*, 2011

CL: I am interested in the genesis of your collaboration for *Two Schools of Cool*. How did the two of you get paired?

ARH: It was the curator Sarah Bancroft's vision. When Sarah spoke to me originally, she hadn't yet selected a partner for me.

CL: Clearly risk is built in to the project.

ARH: True. Sarah described it as a laboratory from the beginning.

CL: Were you familiar with Al's work?

ARH: Of course.

CL: Al, were you familiar with Amanda's work?

AR: Yes. I saw the *New Photography 2010* exhibition at MoMA at about the same time we were having our initial conversations. Amanda's work stuck in my mind, so when Sarah suggested her as a possible collaborator, it was an easy choice. There was one thing that really stood out about her installation—the Peg-Board.

CL: I was getting to that. You have Peg-Board in common, but there's a big difference. The Peg-Board you use, Al, is off the shelf, whereas you made yours, Amanda. Explain why you opted to laboriously drill holes rather than just buying Peg-Board.

ARH: The first time I used Peg-Board in a major work was in the installation I made for the 2008 Whitney Biennial. I had been fascinated with the conceptual implications of Peg-Board for a long time. In that show I wanted to do something in which I acknowledged the temporal context, and for me the Peg-Board is about designating a space that's not fixed. Al, I think you use it for that reason too.

AR: Somewhat, yes.

CL: Because it lends itself to flexibility?

ARH: There is variability, yes. Also, a space in motion correlates to the way I use collage or produce exhibitions or installations. I wanted to do something that was particularly intimate, to create an invasive but also delicate connection with the space. The idea was to transform the room within which I housed a series of objects and images. Once the vocabulary was established, I was able to adapt the use of Peg-Board to small pieces, but I wouldn't have gotten there if I hadn't done that show.

CL: It wasn't the actual labor that was important?

ARH: No, the laborious process of drilling every single hole, entering every single space, was a way to become intimate with it and the architecture.

CL: Al, in your case you use Peg-Board so that images suspended on it can be moved around, but it also has a historical reference. Once ubiquitous, Peg-Board isn't used as much as it once was; it is going out of style.

AR: That's true. But one difference between us is that I import things into the gallery and Amanda tends to make the gallery function architecturally.

ARH: Sometimes, yes. We both search for systems to deal with the impossibility of excess—of finding a place for things even if they are random particles. My Peg-Board works are not variable. At the stage you encounter them, you can't rearrange the objects or images on them as you can with some of Al's. Rather, they function as paused moments in the flux of things moving through a space.

CL: You also share an interest in material culture, in putting things together from varying sources. But whereas Al likes to go to swap meets and garage sales, you, Amanda, are more likely to look on the Internet.

ARH: Yes, especially eBay.

AR: I delegate eBay buying to somebody of Amanda's generation. It saves me from buying things I shouldn't be buying.

CL: Another thing I was wondering about, speaking of generational difference, is how younger artists relate to the general political and cultural climate of our time. When the first generation of conceptual artists emerged in the late 1960s and early 1970s, they felt themselves to be part of a broad political and cultural shift.

ARH: That's a huge question.

CL: This era is characterized by globalization, economically and culturally. Today more information is exchanged more quickly than ever before. I wonder how that affects you, Amanda.

ARH: Even though some of the concerns I have definitely find root in the investigations of Al's generation, the level of access in terms of material culture is totally different–the availability, the ability to search through information–it's a totally different landscape. Al and I talk about a generational divide in terms of what we do and how to parse out our sensibilities. We are still embroiled in that conversation. We have impulses that are almost identical in some cases but also clear generational hiccups.

AR: The space and time between then and now are so enormous. Material culture itself is so different.

ARH: We do have a responsibility, though, to look back at that earlier generation. It's difficult–how can you make work under that crush of history? There is a danger in becoming bogged down. I don't think about it consciously as I am working, but I try to be aware without being oppressed.

AR: That's very different because we were very much aware of being involved in a continuum, aware of the parameters and how they related to history.

CL: You say you were working along a continuum, albeit a short one, but you were also inventing things, entirely new forms.

AR: That was part of the agenda.

ARH: All of my primary gestures are still secondary. I envy the idea that you could make a primary gesture. As much immediacy as I embed in something, I am still aware of the fact that it exists under this crush of the past. It's really tricky; it keeps me motivated because it's a constant challenge.

AR: It's the same thing in music and many other cultural forms of today. Those breaks happen only a couple of times a century–the 1960s, of course, and a lot of influences came from the 1920s. For example, Duchamp became important to the artists of the 1960s. We were there at the right time to pick that up.

CL: You both use family photos. In your case, Amanda, it's often your family. Al, in your case, it's not.

AR: There are exceptions.

CL: But in general your photos are more generic.

AR: But that material was generated from family photographs. I can't use my family pictures because they are too…

CL: Charged…

AR: Too charged. So I extrapolate to others.

CL: You both also reject the idea of nostalgia in your work.

ARH: That's true.

CL: But you do look to the past, Amanda, when you appropriate images of doilies and macramé. Are you interested in craft and its association with women's work?

ARH: No, that's an inevitable association, but really those pieces are about translation from pictures. I like the idea of one level of remove and try to acknowledge it and be clear that there is a loss in the translation. For these works I use images from textile books from the 1960s and 1970s. It's less about history or cultural specificity and more about an interest in pictures of how to make handmade things, things that are not rarefied. I am taking images of made objects and translating them back into being made again. In that sense it's important that they are craft objects, because craft needs to meet craft. I project the photographs, draw them out, paint and hand-cut them, creating a silhouette–a picture and an object simultaneously. I am interested in what you can access in a removed position from these objects. Nothing is made from something I can hold in my hand–it's more about what I can find in the space of objective photography.

CL: What brought you to Los Angeles from Chicago–graduate school?

ARH: Yes. I didn't expect to end up in Los Angeles; I thought it would be New York. I applied to schools on both coasts, but USC had the best program for me, the best deal, and that's where I went. At first I was terrified because I had visited Los Angeles only twice, whereas I had spent a lot of time in New York and could see myself there easily; that was the plan. But I am glad I came here.

CL: One of the liberating concepts that came out of the 1960s was that artists needn't be tied to a specific medium. Rather, the idea should dictate the form. Amanda, you work in several media. You make objects, drawings, photographs.

ARH: I don't do much drawing, but I am not afraid of it.

AR: The one thing I don't do is make paintings.

ARH: You might not pick up a brush, but there are imagistic concerns in your work that refer to painting.

AR: Well, yes.

CL: Had either of you collaborated with another artist before you began working on this project?

ARH: I did an installation using my father's work as material. That's the closest I came to collaboration, but this is my first true collaboration.

AR: I did two collaborations before. Once Larry Johnson gave me some of his prints, and I added something to them. The second time was three or four years ago with my friend Allan McCollum, whom I have known since we were starting out. The works we were making at the time kind of fell together. This is obviously different—two artists who didn't know each other before, starting from scratch.

CL: The proposal must have been intriguing because you both agreed to do it.

ARH: I was thrilled and immediately had ideas about what we had in common. One thing we share is an interest in a particular tone of voice, a vernacular poetic based on found language that can embody multiple meanings and open-ended references. Al, I was really struck with your banner that said "Everything is collected nothing is saved." Before seeing that, I had made a banner that said something similar: "We can't get enough because there's too much."

CL: How have you proceeded?

ARH: At first we were busy and traveling, e-mailing each other all over the world. In fact, I thought our remote conversation might inform the project, but finally our paths aligned so that we could meet face-to-face. We did some very early studio visit exchanges to get a sense of how we each maneuver within our spaces. That was critical for ideas to start brewing. Our work spaces are very different—I have one space, not two, and we have different kinds of things in our spaces. But we are both interested in the archive and how we arrange our collections. I have a lot of flat files, random bins, and drawers, and a lot in the computer.

AR: That's very different, because my archives are not in a computer to begin with. When they are, they have already been somewhere else first.

ARH: There's a physical index somewhere else.

AR: Right.

CL: Do you want to talk about what you are planning to do together?

AR: We have a structure and a title, *The Meaning of Plus and Minus*, that comes from an old educational film I own.

ARH: Even before the idea of the piece became more concrete, we decided that it was a brilliant title for a collaborative work.

CL: It's a great title because it can be read on many different levels.

ARH: Yes, it suggests many things I deal with, such as positive and negative space, adding and subtracting, and it describes what we are physically trying to do.

AR: It also refers to past and present, relationships.

CL: Are you going to make something ahead of time or work in the space together?

AR: We are making an object. From the start we agreed that what we create should be very simple and not refer to ideas that people might have about each of our practices.

ARH: It should be something that distills our sensibilities into one but also subverts expectations. People might expect us to create a sprawling installation with Peg-Board, for example, but that was definitely on the list Al made of "things we cannot do." Furthermore, we agreed that in the resulting work it wouldn't be easy to discern whose hand made what.

AR: Yes, the seams shouldn't be visible.

CL: It won't be interactive?

AR: No. It will be an object that can go into the world by itself.

CL: Can you think of anything you would like to say that I haven't asked you? Is this going to be the beginning of something big?

ARH: ...a beautiful friendship. I hope so. Getting to know Al has been a treat for me. It's really inspiring to be in conversation with someone whose practice is so important and broad.

AR: An unexpected but beneficial outcome of the collaboration is the realization that you can't help but introduce ideas that you have been thinking about in other contexts and that will go somewhere else after the collaboration.

ARH: That's true for me as well, as opposed to the collaboration being extracurricular.

CL: Thank you both. I can't wait to see the exhibition.

Overleaf:
Installation view with Amanda Ross-Ho and Allen Ruppersberg, *The Meaning of Plus and Minus*, 2011 (left, foreground), and Shana Lutker and John Baldessari, *A -> B*, 2011 (right, background)

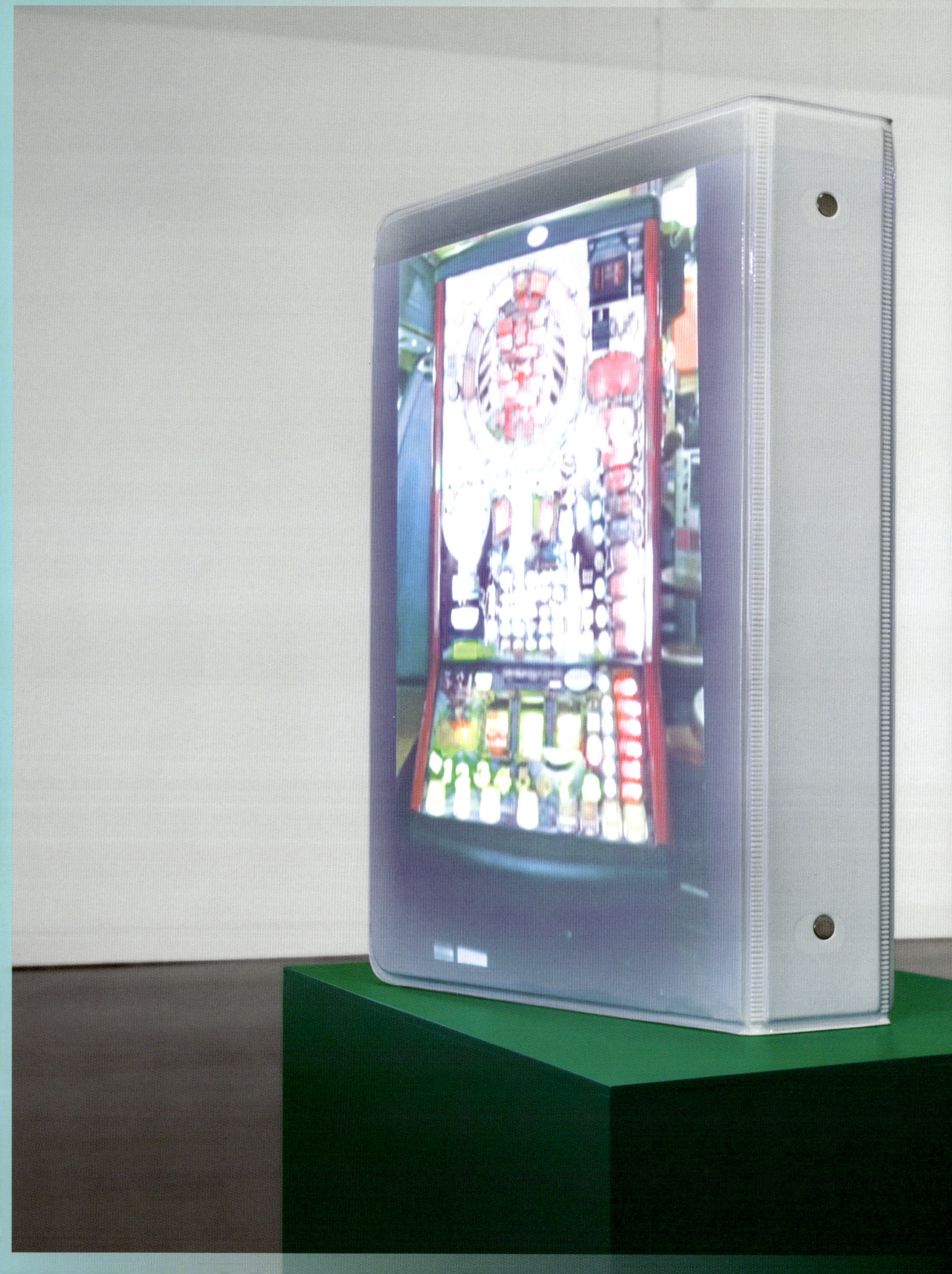

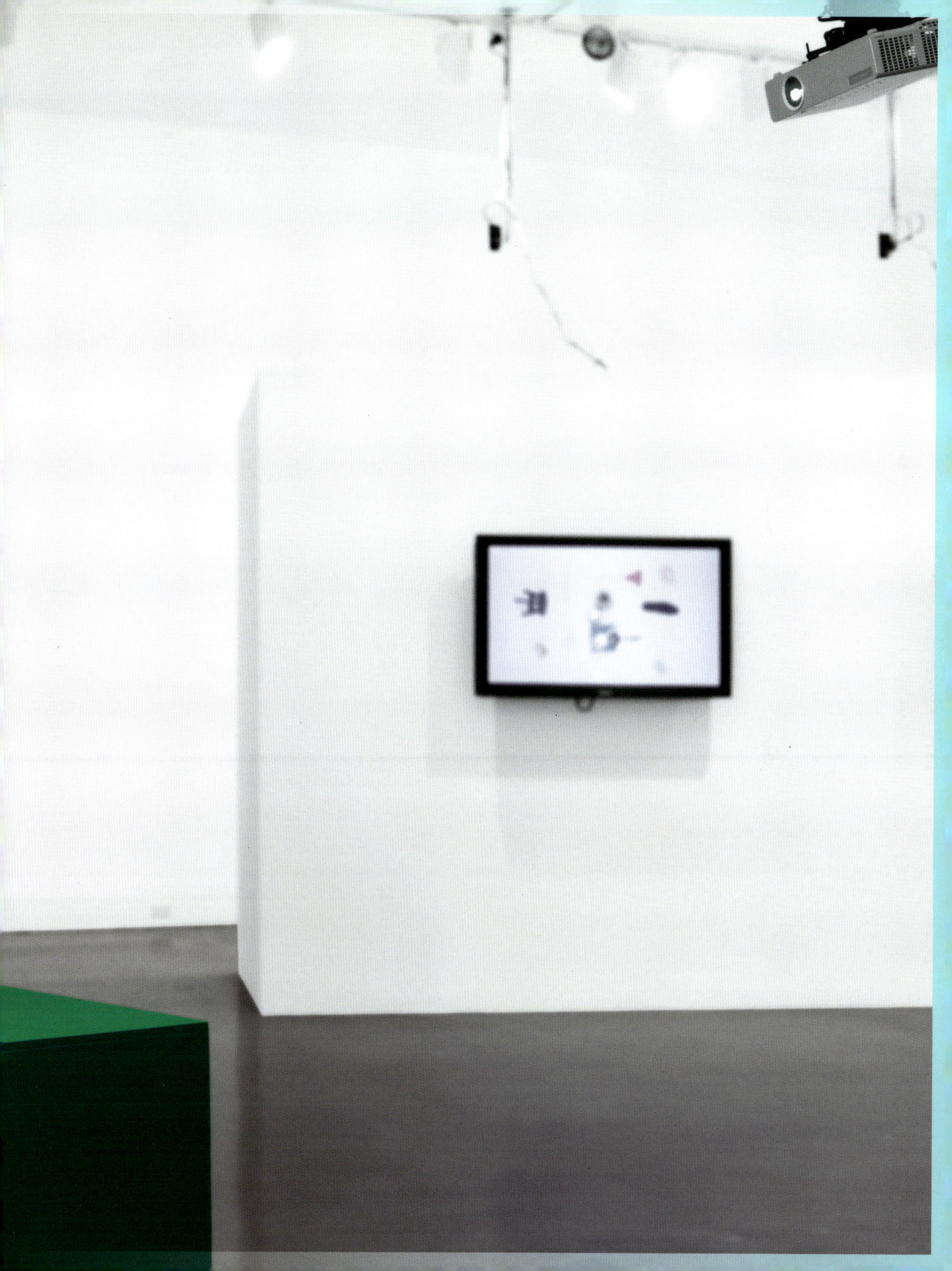

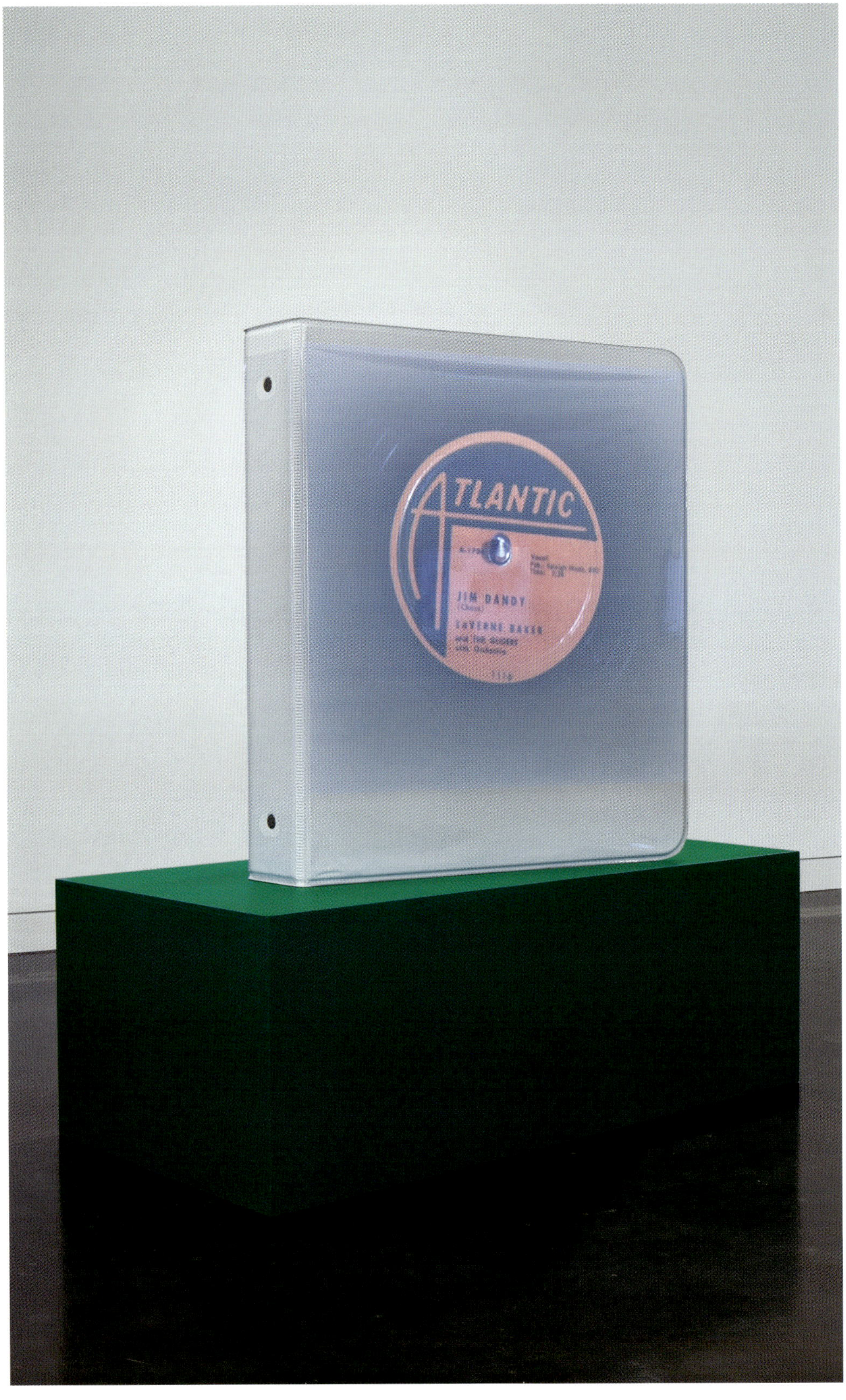

Amanda Ross-Ho and
Allen Ruppersberg
The Meaning of Plus and Minus, 2011
(installation view with moving-image projection)

Amanda Ross-Ho and
Allen Ruppersberg
The Meaning of Plus and Minus, 2011
(detail of binder)

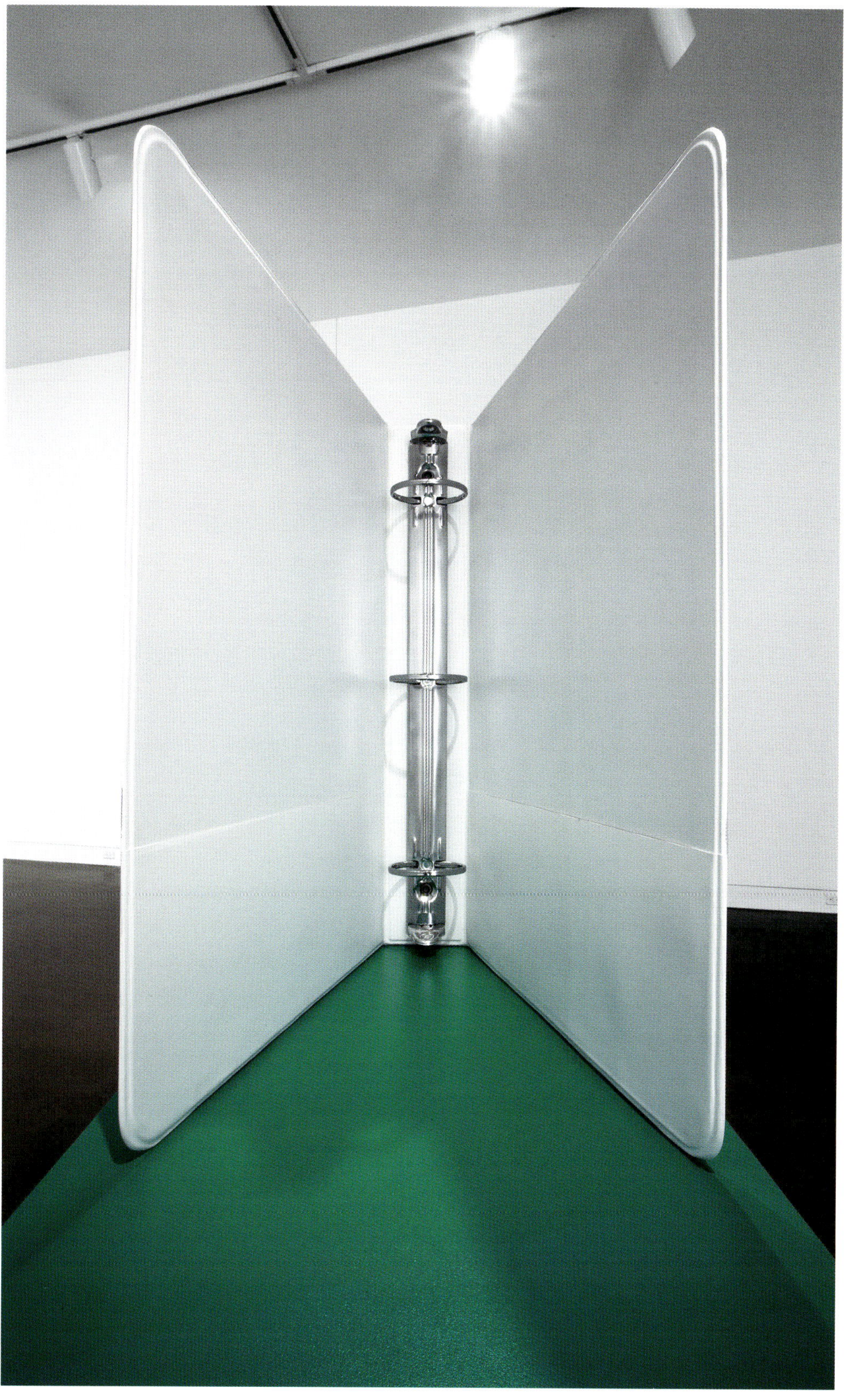

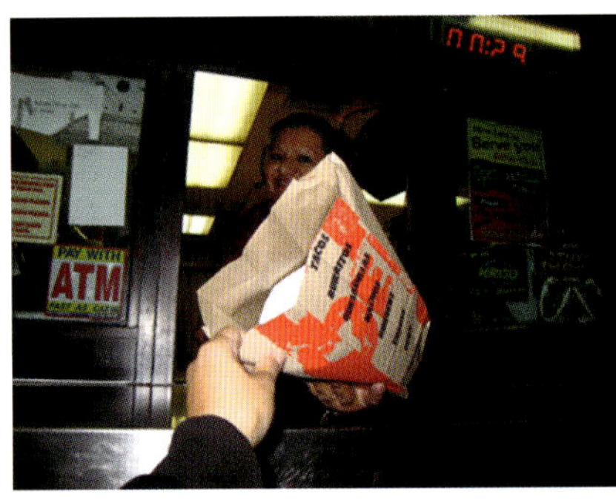

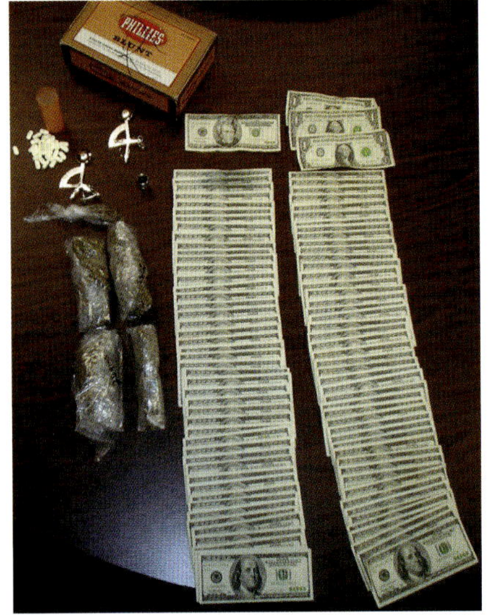

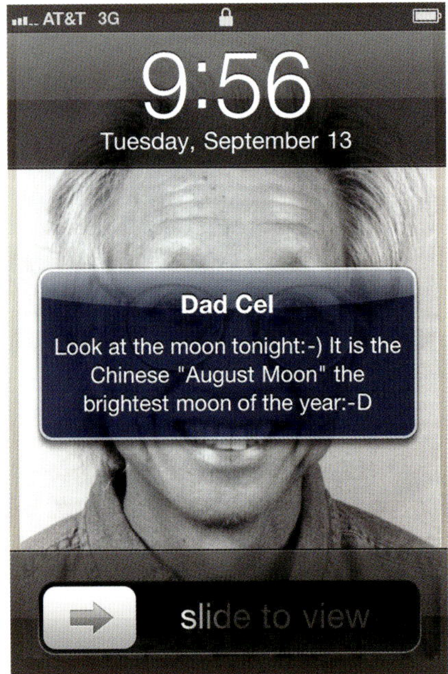

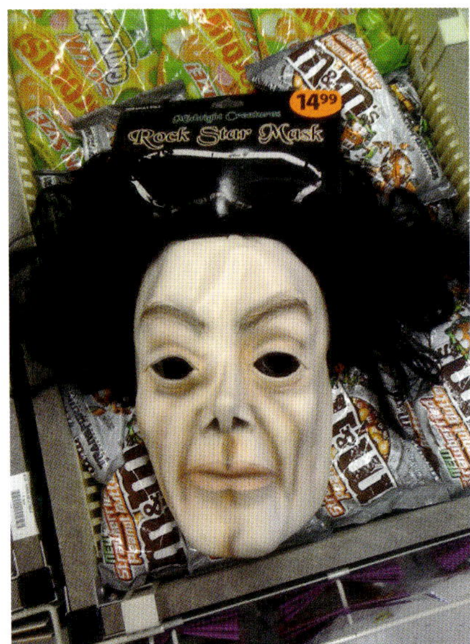

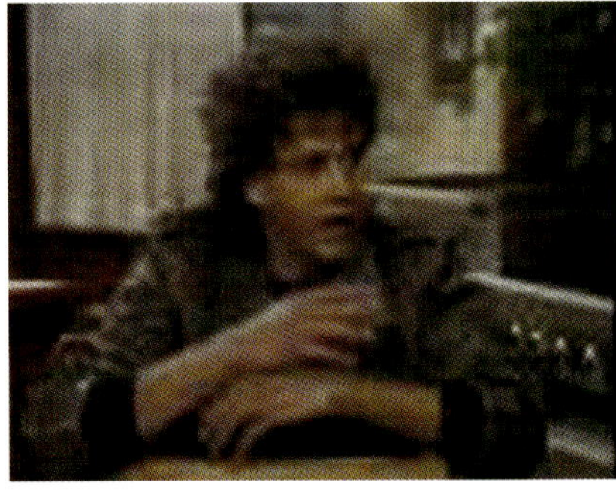

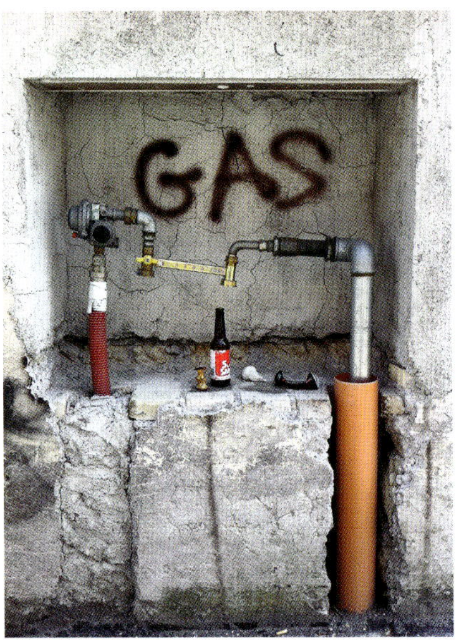

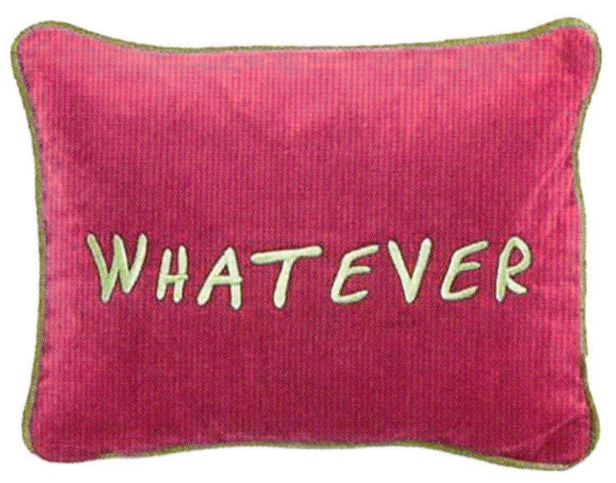

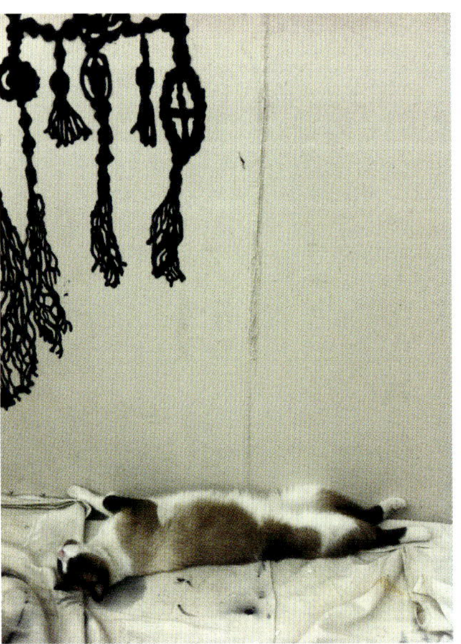

Amanda Ross-Ho and Allen Ruppersberg
The Meaning of Plus and Minus, 2011
(selections from digital slide show of images from Amanda Ross-Ho's archive)

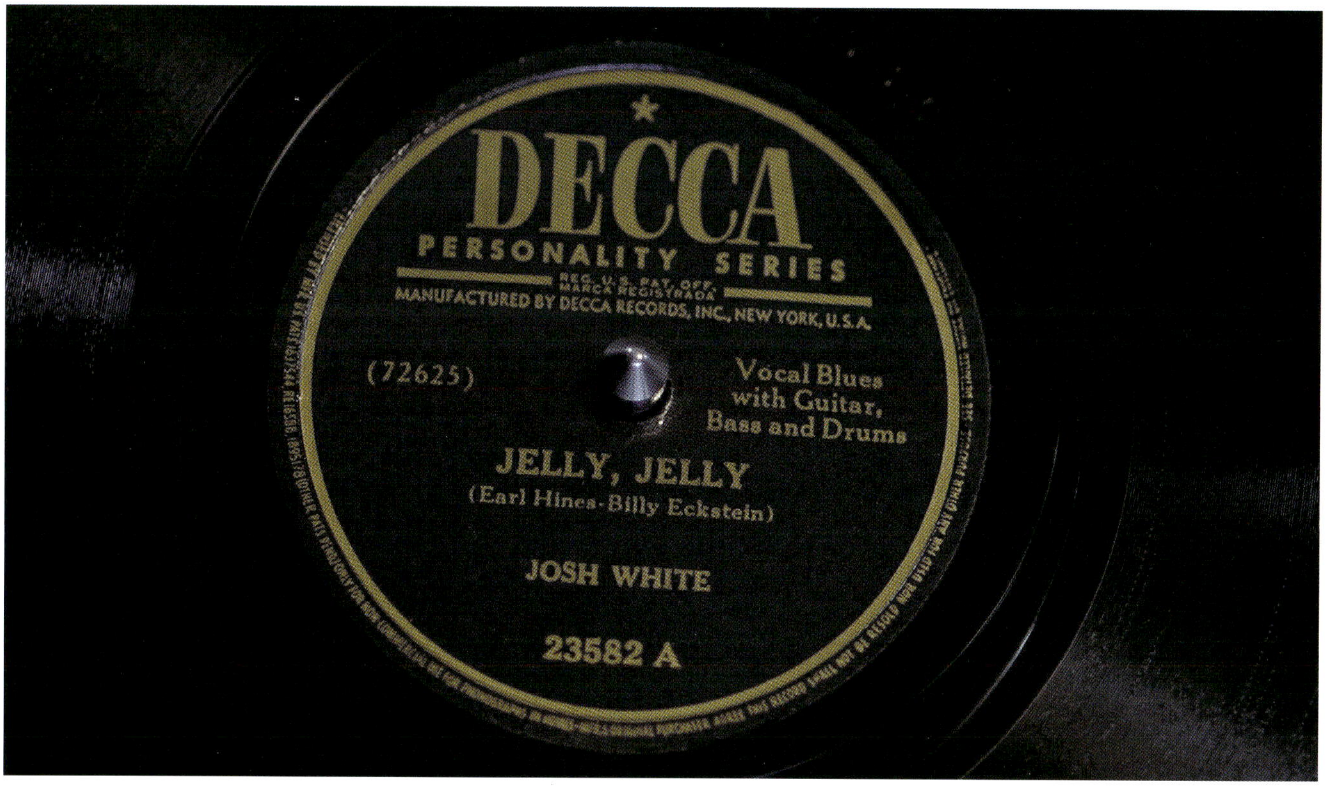

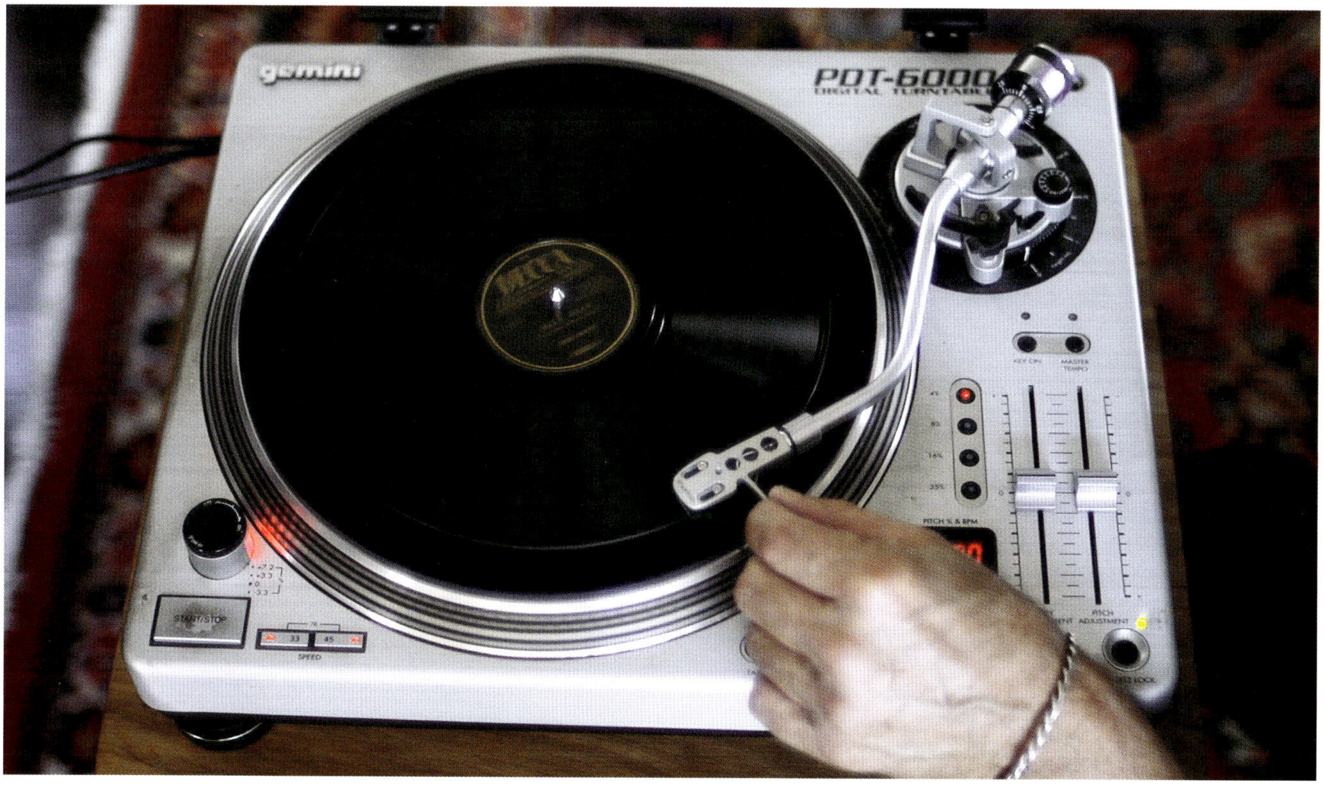

Amanda Ross-Ho and Allen Ruppersberg
The Meaning of Plus and Minus, 2011
(stills from moving-image projection of 78s from Allen Ruppersberg's archive)

ROBERT WILLIAMS AND ED MOSES

For this collaboration, Robert Williams and Ed Moses, who share a mutual admiration, have each selected paintings from the other's recent body of work, and each artist has written wall label texts that encapsulate his thoughts about and collegial critiques of his colleague's work. This installation brings together disparate works in a compelling fashion, highlighting the formal differences between Moses's and Williams's paintings by alternating the works on the walls. (Williams's paintings are hung on a vertical gray stripe, and Moses's are unframed on the bare white walls.) Moses became part of the Los Angeles art establishment in the early 1960s, exhibiting at the seminal Ferus Gallery, which opened in 1957, and creating an ever-evolving body of work over the last fifty years. Williams first became known for his contributions to Zap Comix in the 1970s, developed a psychedelic painterly style in the 1980s, and was the founder of *Juxtapoz* magazine in 1994. His highly detailed and cartoonlike compositions presenting salacious story lines and provocative scenarios, as well as his equally notable record cover designs for numerous rock bands, have assured his position as a cult hero of the artistic counterculture. This collaborative presentation speaks to the artists' distinct audiences and to the more abstract versus the overtly graphic nature of their respective practices. The paintings created by these art icons reflect the rich diversity of the Los Angeles art scene.

Installation view with Robert Williams, *Creation Trumps Creator*, 2010 (left), and Ed Moses, *Dance of the Snake*, 2011 (right)

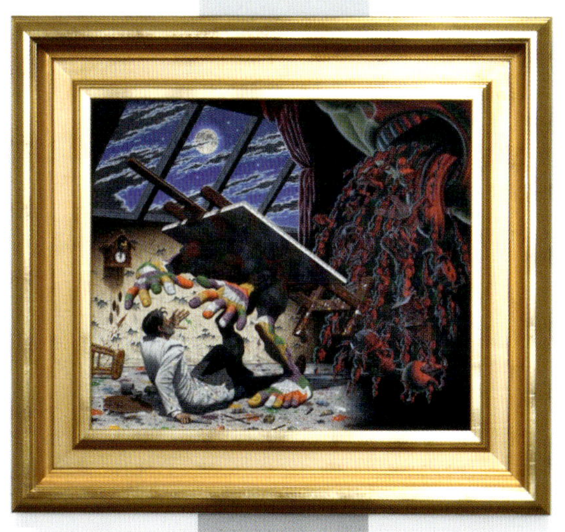
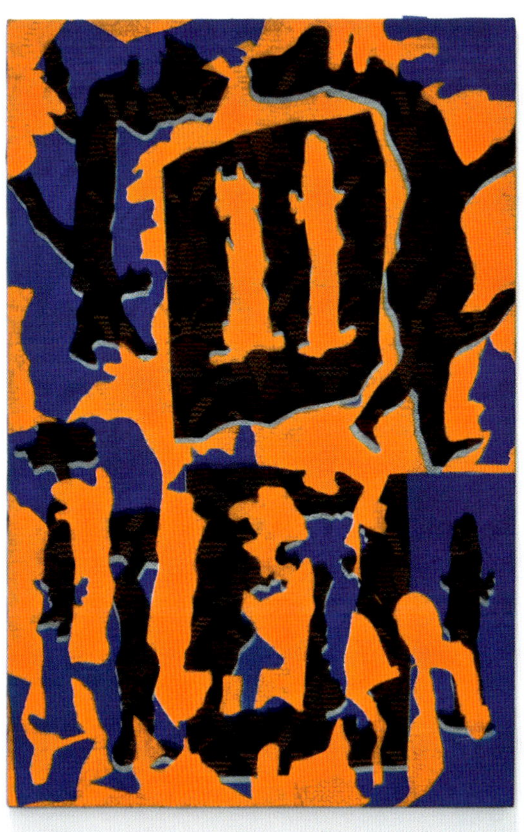

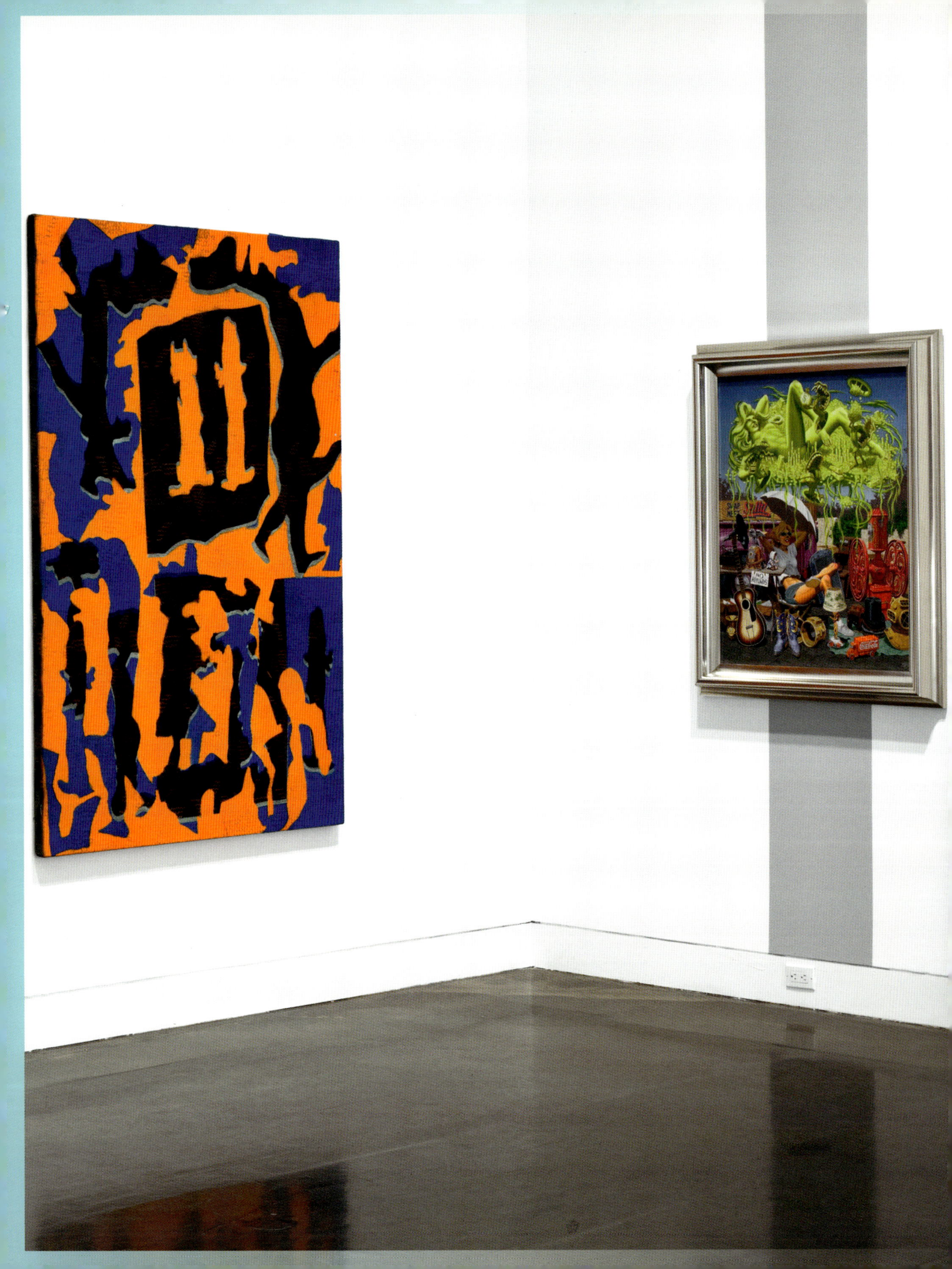

Robert Williams and Ed Moses

Interview by Sarah C. Bancroft and Andy Moses

Installation view with Ed Moses, *Dance of the Snake*, 2011 (left), and Robert Williams, *Swap Meet Sally*, 2005 (right)

SB: Here's an image of Bob's [Robert Williams's] painting *Swap Meet Sally*.

EM: What strikes me about Bob's paintings is that they're contemporaneous in terms of the culture. But if you look through a mirror, you would see that this, this top part, this is one side, and this is the other side [points to bottom of the painting]. So I think everything we do is bifurcated. In other words, there's two sides.

When I was driving across the country many years ago, I stopped in a little thrift store, and on the wall they had this piece of stone about eight by twelve inches; two inches thick almost. I don't know why I picked it up. I was just fascinated... and I always thought about it as a mirror. Jorge Luis Borges talks about a stone mirror, which is a kind of metaphor for the other side. Bob's paintings fit right into this thinking, like the garden of forking paths. And I think Bob is into that but not consciously; none of us are conscious when we are doing it.... What I like about him is that he can carefully execute and render images that he intuits. (I don't know how he comes up with these paintings, but I'm just talking about how I respond to them.)

SB: It's perceptive, you speaking of the two-sidedness. Here's Sally, and above, this is her dream, I think, what will come for her, the riches.

EM: Or it's not even her dreams; it's just the other side of her being.

RW: I spend a lot of time at different kinds of swap meets. I enjoy them because the part of your character that's the rapacious hunter gets to search. The swap meet or the flea market is one of the last examples of the true marketplace, the ancient marketplace. The other characteristic [of the painting] is the girl in it, the pulchritude. Marketplaces used to be the places where you'd meet females, members of the opposite sex. She's not just watching the stall for her dad while he's gone; she's actually the horse trader. She knows what she's got, and nothing's going to get by her. And you can see at the top, on that side of the deal, the corrupting character of both money and sex.

EM: So you do have literal meanings behind the images that you choose and execute?

RW: I do; I go overboard with it. Not only is there too much detail and too much written into it, but I can verbally bore you to death about this painting. Most of the stuff in here, a lot of it I made up, like the giant coffee grinder and the hula girl and the lamp, and I made up the Coca-Cola truck and the boots...

EM: Did you take a photograph of this particular setting?

RW: No, no... I do not use photographs; I do not appropriate photography.

EM: Even for recording, you don't?

RW: I use photography for studying, never for appropriating. I get down to dividers and figure out perspective and you know. It's a mental illness. It's an obsession. [*Laughter.*]

EM: I understand.

RW: And it's long past the point of me trying to entertain the people. It's such an obsession that it's me entertaining myself.

AM: I started to think about the connectors between you guys, because at first glance your work is very, very different. One of them would be obsession. All artists are obsessive, but you take it to another level.

RW: In my opinion, the most interesting point between my work and Ed's is how extremely different [it is], not only visually but in terms of philosophy and time period.

EM: I'd agree with that. You know, [Bob's] an alien to me. I have certain people that are in my tribe. And when I first met Bob through Ed Ruscha, I felt a kind of aggression and power that made me uncomfortable.

SB: When you say an aggression, do you mean his work or Bob as a person?

EM: His persona, the energy he exudes as a human being, is an hombre. [*Laughter.*] And he ain't taking any shit.

RW: You know, I was and still am an underground cartoonist who came out of the sixties, when I worked heavily with Zap Comix in San Francisco and I was an anarchist and pornographer. I resented any kind of graphic authority, and when I got in with other cartoonists, underground cartoonists, I realized that they had the same problem in art schools that I had. I came up in the early sixties through art school, Los Angeles City College and Chouinard, and I was taught that realism was dead and over; it was dead and fucking over.

EM: That's right.

RW: And it appealed only to people with "weak mentalities" to use realism as a crutch, you see.

EM: I didn't get that one.

RW: I tried very hard in school to develop a taste and appreciation for [nonrepresentational art]. You [Ed] are an extension of that taste and appreciation. I came to grips with it, and I understood it, but I still had the compulsion to think in three and four dimensions. So it was me and just a handful of people who stood totally alone with representational art. Except illustrators.

EM: So you were an isolated phenomenon, you were out there apart?

RW: Well, I appreciate you noticing. [*Laughter.*]

EM: Well, you're stating that; I don't agree with that. I want to understand where you're coming from.

AM: And when did you become aware of that schism, of the so-called fine art world, L.A. art world, Ferus Gallery?

RW: I was always there; I always went to La Cienega on Monday nights.

AM: But most of your peers, I mean, you did have a peer group; they just weren't in the L.A. "art world."

RW: No, they were underground cartoonists.

AM: Exactly. So they didn't seem so intent on showing at galleries?

RW: They all went to art school too and, like me, reverted back to comic book graphics.

AM: But you think some of your peers were happier just staying in the world of underground comics and custom car culture? Those two worlds were very separate [from the fine art world] back then, and now there's a lot of crossover.

RW: There's an awful lot of crossover. Things have really changed.

SB: That's one reason I wanted you in the show, because there is a focus on and fascination with the Ferus Gallery in Los Angeles, which is telling only part of the story…

EM: Right, very small.

SB: Yeah, and I have a connection to Walter [Hopps], yet there are other moments in L.A. history beyond the Ferus Gallery that I'm trying to fish out. Ed comes from the establishment of the L.A. art world really, and Bob's history is quite different yet equally significant. Ed, you were mentioning that although Bob sees himself on the outside, you don't. So where do you see him?

EM: Well, I just saw him as an exceptional artist, but he didn't fit into what I knew, which I always like. Before, I was a rigid abstract painter; I still have a couple of friends who are solid in the belief that abstract painting is it, that's it. Later on, I realized that was a joke. I moved out and around [abstraction], and that's why I consider myself from "the garden of forking paths." It's a labyrinth, it has no beginning or end, and it certainly has no meaning. So when I look at Bob's work, there's a kind of mythical thing with the culture and with the "other side" that intrigues me. But I can't give it meaning. I have a hard time giving anything meaning.

RW: Let me put it like this: abstract art has an enormous poetic voice, an abstract poetic voice. But realism has got a much larger vocabulary. So the two have to coexist no matter what.

EM: They do, whether we want it or not.

RW: Well, I want it, and I would certainly come to your defense under any circumstance. It's important to me that you have freedom so that I can have freedom at the other end.

AM: [Ed,] I know you resist or don't like the label of freedom, but in your work you're certainly beholden to nobody, and in spite of what everyone tells you to do, you always do whatever you want.

EM: So that has a kind of freedom in it?

AM: I think that's the definition of *freedom*, and I don't think *freedom* has to be a dirty word. It just allows you to follow your own obsession or exploration or investigation and not pay attention to what the world is telling you to do, and I think both of you guys have that sense of independence. *Independence* may be a better word than *freedom*.

EM: Well, *freedom* is sort of political.

AM: *Freedom* is like a dirty word now! [*Laughter.*] And you're doing paintings now that many of your abstract cohorts would find very distasteful.

EM: Oh, they don't like 'em.

AM: And you're working from these places of sort of pop cultural imagery because it's coming from fabrics and faces even though you're using it in a very different way.

EM: Yeah, and cartoons.

SB: Yes, when Bob chose those four paintings from your studio for the show, I thought, *Wow, there is a through line between your works.* As crazy as that sounds. You're clearly bastardizing cartoon figures in the work and abstracting them in some way. It relates so directly to Bob's work in a way that I never would have imagined, because I don't put the two of you in the same category. You are a pairing of opposites, really.

EM: Well, I'd never done that before, and what was interesting is that I doodle at my desk. And I noticed many years ago that I started doing these heads facing each other, with their tongues touching in real aggressive kinds of gestures, and then I finally transmitted them to canvases, which I drew with enamel with a stick, and then I poured paint on one side and squeegeed across so it erased and dismembered this drawing, because I've never considered myself an adequate draftsman on any level. It wasn't until I took some classes from Howard Warshaw that I could even draw in three dimensions. Some guys, like [Bob] and Kenny Price, could do cartoons and they did wonderful things, and I was always jealous that they could do that, and I did airplanes in two dimensions on boards or whatever. So we are sort of antithetical.

SB: You're the two sides.

EM: Well, I don't know what we're the two sides of! [*Laughter.*] The phenomenal world?

RW: There was a period when abstract expressionism absolutely ruled the Western world. When I was going to art school, I was taught that when you use paint, it's got to look like paint, and it's gotta be messy. That's the true nature of the material. When you're an artist, you have to be honest. If you carve in stone, you have to show the chisel marks; if you use a torch, you've got to burn the metal up. This is being "true to your medium." If you tried to do things too realistically, then you were trying to trick. I was in a lecture class in the early sixties, and the teacher was showing slides, and he showed Rubens's *Descent from the Cross*, big famous painting, great painting. And the teacher said: "This is not an oil painting. This is a colored-in drawing." And I knew I was in trouble right there; I knew I wasn't with the program. You couldn't be a realist. I was taught in art school, do not have any converging lines because it suggests perspective.

EM: Is that right? Who were your teachers then?

RW: Oh, god, I can't remember. Anyway, there is a great deal of realism where we are now. People are questioning…

EM: I agree; I finally gave up [abstraction].

AM: So, Sarah, this is your project. What brought these two artists together in your mind?

EM: Was that your decision that we would dance together?

SB: It was. And originally I'd paired each of you with another artist, a younger artist, trying to get people from different generations to work together. Although technically you two are not from the same generation (so you do fit the definition of *intergenerational*). Yours is the "unlikely" pairing in the show. The exhibition is a lab and a forum for possibility.

EM: You know, I was recently reading that guy in Las Vegas, Dave Hickey, and he talks about why be afraid of beauty. He loves beautiful things and beauty, and I always wanted to be [making] tough paintings and not pretty paintings. But in spite of that I always did beautiful paintings; I always had a great color sense. Just automatically: I mean, I didn't think "which color's gonna go there?" I just did it. And I think [Bob's] paintings indicate that kind of thinking too. I don't know whether you move along as you paint or you have a plan and more or less [know] what you're going to do.

RW: Well, it's all worked out in the drawings. So when it goes onto the canvas, there's a little ad-libbing and a little change when I see mistakes in perspective and anatomy and stuff and certain folds in the clothes.

EM: So it's like a classic Renaissance artist.

RW: I'm afraid it is, yeah.

EM: Where the art was mapped out and had cartoons. They were usually on paper, the [Renaissance] cartoons, right?

RW: Yeah, vellum.

EM: Now the interior of this tent [in the painting *In the Pavilion of the Red Clown* (2001)], you just imagined it?

RW: Everything in that picture, I imagined. The wine bottles, everything.

EM: Now is that a temporal thing, spread out over a period of time?

RW: No, I just sit down, and think, I wanna get this sonofabitch done…

EM: So you start moving with your imagination, right there when you're drawing?

RW: Yeah. Just like comic book art, [there's] very little reference in there. In that particular painting, there is no reference. It's just me doing so many paintings [that] I know what I wanted.

EM: By no reference, you mean previous things.

RW: Yeah, I don't copy anything; the faces don't represent anything. They're just stylizations.

EM: See, my reaction is that I could never do anything like that. I'm amazed that somebody can do it. I don't see any brushstrokes, so how did you get the paint on there? Is it with a gun or did you blend it?

RW: A brush, it's done in a number of ways…

EM: Well, it's great to be sitting here looking at that painting, a beautiful thing, and then I jump-cut to how did he do it? You're here performing with words what you're doing, and then I look at this and don't see that at all. So it's a hard transmission.

RW: You're seeing it technically through the eyes of an artist. That picture would be for someone hung up on what's in it. In other words, the character of that clown isn't a nice guy. He's a drunk, he's disabled, and he's putting the make on that gal that he's talked into coming back here in the tent with him, and he's having a great deal of pleasure showing her that that bird got eaten by that snake. [*Laughter.*] It's close to a pulp magazine cover; it has that cheap sensationalism about it.

EM: And you like that?

RW: I love that, I love that; that's my art. There's a word for it: it's called meretricious. That means it's so shitty, it's so tacky, that it's an art form. [*Laughter.*]

EM: I see, uh-huh. I was wondering if you knew that. [*Laughter.*]

SB: On that note, when did you decide that you were going to be a "fine art" painter?

RW: I admit to being a fine painter in my late teens. I did my first oil painting when I was fourteen, in 1957, but I seriously came out to California to be a "fine art" artist in '63. I had all these ideas of hot rod art, pulp magazines, and naked ladies, and the first school I go to is Los Angeles City College, and I realize that I'm right in the middle of the AbEx movement and I don't have a hope in hell. So then I went to Chouinard for a while and learned some graphics, and then I had to get a job. So I got a job as the art director at *Black Belt* magazine. They fired me. I got a job as a container designer at Weyerhaeuser Corporation, and they fired me. This is during my psychedelic period. [*Laughter.*] Finally I got a job with Ed "Big Daddy" Roth. He looked at my work, and he says, "If I'd known you existed, I'd have hunted you up." So I became his art director and started making a ton of money for five years, and while I was doing that, I went back to painting, you see. And while I was working at Roth's, I met one of his competitors, a guy named Stanley Mouse, one of the big five who started the psychedelic poster movement. And through him I met Rick Griffin, and I met the guys who started Zap Comix in San Francisco, so I asked for pages, and they said, "Sure, we love your stuff."

SB: Have either of you collaborated before?

RW: No.

EM: No. Never imagined how I would collaborate. That's my feeling. There's no way. But maybe with a little thought and a little time and play, that could happen.

AM: I like your work shown together because it will fight in a good way; your work already fights with whomever looks at it, and that fighting with each other and with the audience will bring an impactful zone into the exhibition.

EM: I hope you're right there, Andy. I don't know. I can't imagine them being in a room, side by side. I can't imagine it is what I'm saying. It's not some moral thing.

SB: Right, you literally can't imagine.

EM: I literally can't imagine.

RW: Morals aren't on the table here. There's no right and wrong, and there's no morals here.

EM: That's right.

• • • • •

For the exhibition, Moses and Williams each selected four recent paintings by the other and developed labels for some of the works (the label texts are reprinted below). They will also engage in a critique of each other's practices in a public program during the exhibition.

Ed Moses
Hed-Owt #3, 2011
This is the painting that would have difficulty being accepted as part of the lobby decor in a mental facility. It's just too psychedelic. It not only takes fortitude to have a background of Pepto-Bismol pink for your imagery—it takes an understanding of color. Ed Moses, over his many years as an artist, developed a remarkable intuition about the use of hue, tone, and value of pigments. This comes with decades of color trial and error. Remember, these works were done fairly quickly, and notice that the irrational and unobtrusive cartoon forms are by no means sedate. These shapes are as overt and aggressive as the magenta background.

This, to me, is an exemplary and stimulating piece of art, but it has the same problem many really wonderful works suffer from. Where would it go without dominating any environment it fell into? The color balance speaks highly of an artist with unconscious natural ability and sixty years experience. Ed Moses is, at very least, a prime example of romantic abstract art history. Ed, I salute you.

—Robt. Williams

Robert Williams
Wrangling the Firmament
Ed Moses: When I met Bob, I saw him as an exceptional artist, but he didn't fit into what I knew, which I liked. Before, I was a rigid abstract painter. Later on, I realized that was a joke. I moved out and around [abstraction], and that's why I consider myself from "the garden of forking paths." It's elaborate, it has no beginning or end, and it certainly has no meaning. So when I look at Bob's work, there's a kind of mythical thing with the culture and with the "other side" that intrigues me. But I can't give it meaning. I have a hard time giving anything meaning.

Robert Williams: Let me put it like this: abstract art has an enormous poetic voice, an abstract poetic voice. But realism has got a much larger vocabulary. So the two have to coexist no matter what.

Ed Moses: Oh, they do. Whether we want it or not.

Robert Williams: Well, I want it, and I would certainly come to your defense under any circumstance. It's important to me that you have freedom so that I can have freedom at the other end.

Ed Moses
Hed-Owt #2, 2011
Not every painting Ed Moses creates is the scream of the imprisoned psyche. *Hed-Owt #2* would add to the pastoral repose of a doctor's office. You can't go wrong with earth colors and maybe a precocious bit of light yellow. However, this work is by no means innocuous. After a little observation, a trained eye will visually match a positive cartoon shape with its negative same-shaped hole—but then only to find that the other corresponding forms don't match anything. If this work had to be classified in the great scheme of the historic art pantheon, it would fit somewhere alongside the art of Franz Kline, John Marin, or Philip Guston. Ed loosely seems to be caught in the purgatory of a postexpressionism with a strong will to still function in an atmosphere of abstract purity. If he falls under the label of abstract expressionist, it should be remembered that abstract expressionist artists are, by serious academic definition, the true romantics. And, in spite of wordy art speak, Ed Moses does paint with his heart.

—Robt. Williams

Ed Moses
Me, 2011
I can only presume that the title *Me* for Ed Moses's 2011 painting refers to himself in some vague abstract second-person or multiple persona, since the images consist of one large character and three similar silhouettes.

Apparently, the real story here is the obtuse nature of the forms. Everything certainly works well on this black fabric field, so Ed speaks clearly here. In fact, all the figures in this set of paintings have been obtained by transferring stencils. So by merely painting and shifting slightly, the repainting causes a shadow image to be created. This second edge gives the impression of dimension. This brilliant little touch lends emotional depth to a normally static graphic.

Also, Ed's design interplay within the forms gives lyricism to the work. The cartoon figures are just indefinable enough to invite the viewer to investigate. This, with a free sense of random placement, keeps the work relaxed and spontaneous.

—Robt. Williams

Ed Moses
Dance of the Snake, 2011
Maybe a dance, but no observable snakes here. Ed Moses has taken visual definition into the world of his own poetry. Ed is an artist who resists typecasting and classification, but still traditional art language does present itself in this painting. He has, in the past, created abbreviated identifiable shapes in his work; however, he has also distinguished himself with remarkable nonobjective paintings that have bordered on purely abstract pattern and design.

In this work Ed has masterfully fused near recognizable forms with bold, unadulterated color, giving the impression that the imagery exists solely to exploit the color contrast. However, the orange and blue hues are marginally quieted with sienna.

—Robt. Williams

Robert Williams
Swap Meet Sally
Ed Moses: What strikes me about Bob's paintings is that they're contemporaneous in terms of the culture. But if you look through a mirror, you would see that this, this top part, this is one side, and this is the other side [points to bottom of the painting]. So I think everything we do is bifurcated. In other words, there's two sides. This is just the other side of her being.

When I was driving across the country many years ago, I stopped in a little thrift store, and on the wall they had this piece of stone about eight by twelve inches; two inches thick almost. I don't know why I picked it up; I was just fascinated… and I always thought about it as a mirror. Jorge Luis Borges talks about a stone mirror, which is a kind of metaphor for the other side. Bob's paintings fit right into this thinking, like the garden of forking paths. And I think Bob is into that but not consciously; none of us are conscious when we are doing it…. What I like about him is that he can carefully execute and render images that he intuits. (I don't know how he comes up with these paintings, but I'm just talking about how I respond to them.)

Robert Williams: I spend a lot of time at swap meets, different kinds of swap meets. I enjoy swap meets because the part of your character that's the rapacious hunter gets to search. The swap meet or the flea market is one of the last examples of the true marketplace, the ancient marketplace. The other characteristic [of the painting] is the girl in it, the pulchritude. Marketplaces used to be the places where you'd meet females, members of the opposite sex. She's not just watching the stall for her dad while he's gone; she's actually a horse trader. She knows what she's got. And you can see at the top [of the painting], you can see the merchandising example, that side of the deal, the corrupting character of both money and sex.

Overleaf:
Installation view with (left to right) Robert Williams, *Gimme, Gimme, Gimme*, 2011; Ed Moses, *Hed-Owt #3*, 2011; Robert Williams, *Wrangling the Firmament*, 2008; Ed Moses, *Hed-Owt #2*, 2011; Ed Moses, *Me*, 2011; Robert Williams, *Creation Trumps Creator*, 2010; and Ed Moses, *Dance of the Snake*, 2011

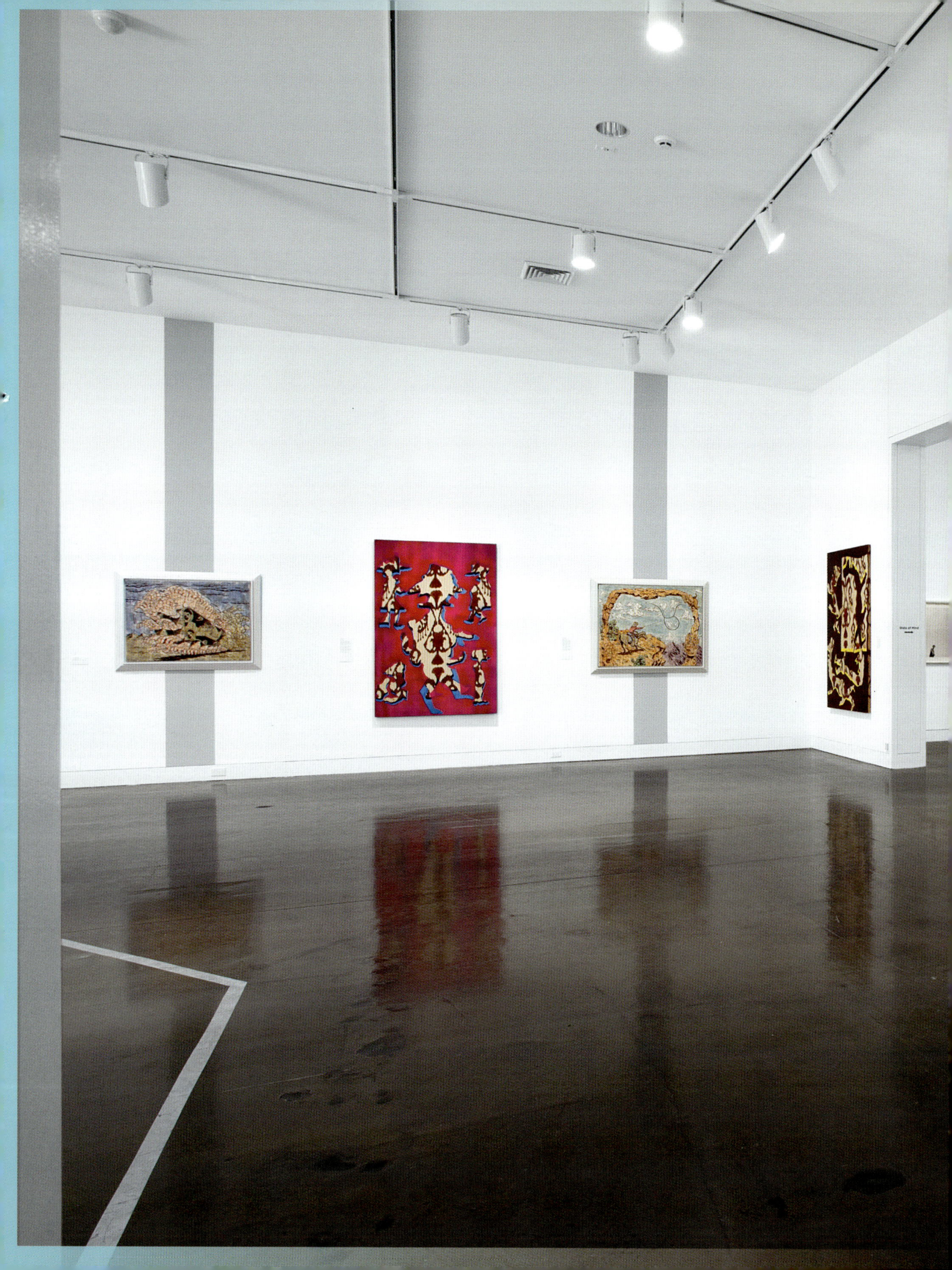

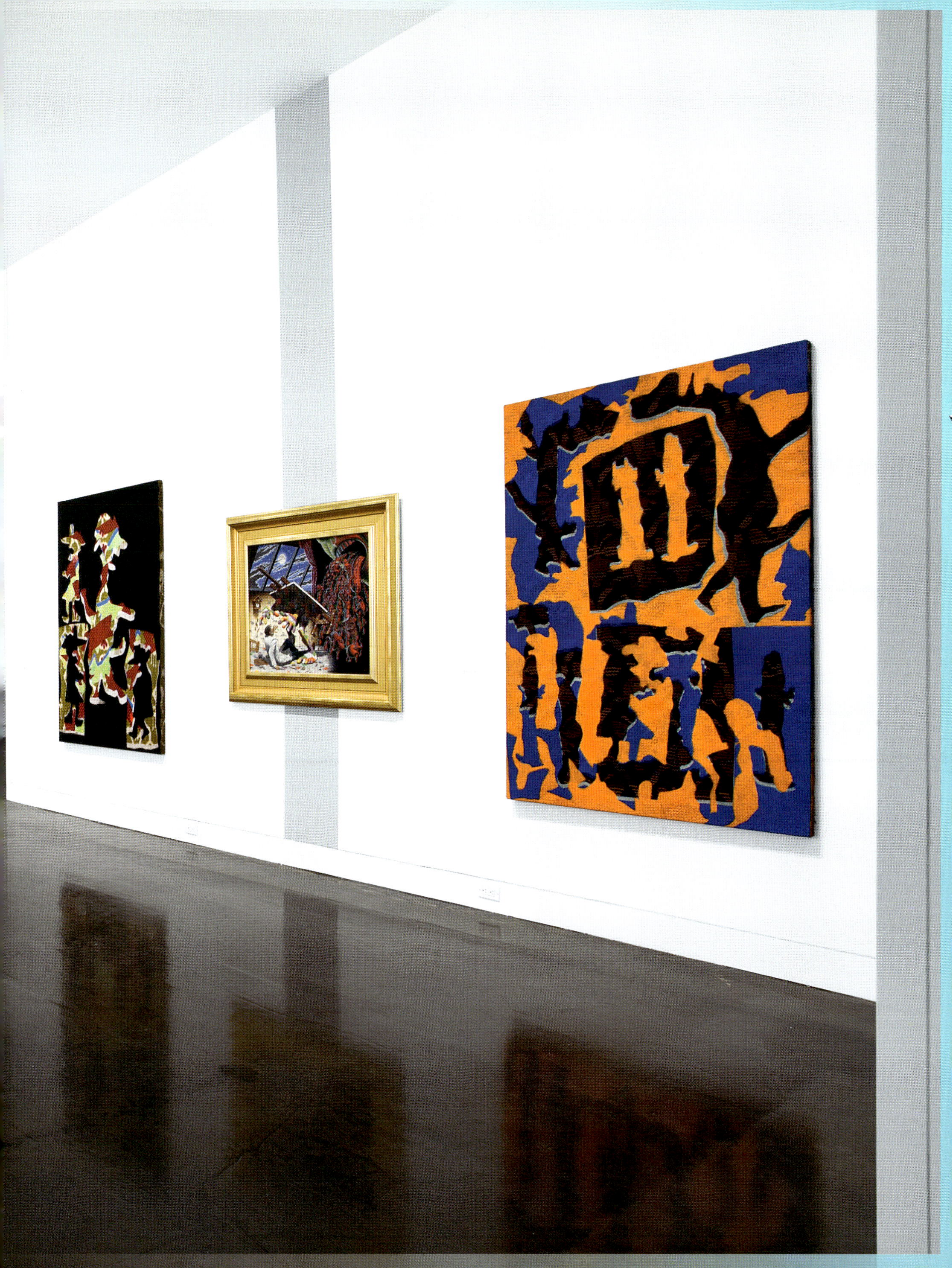

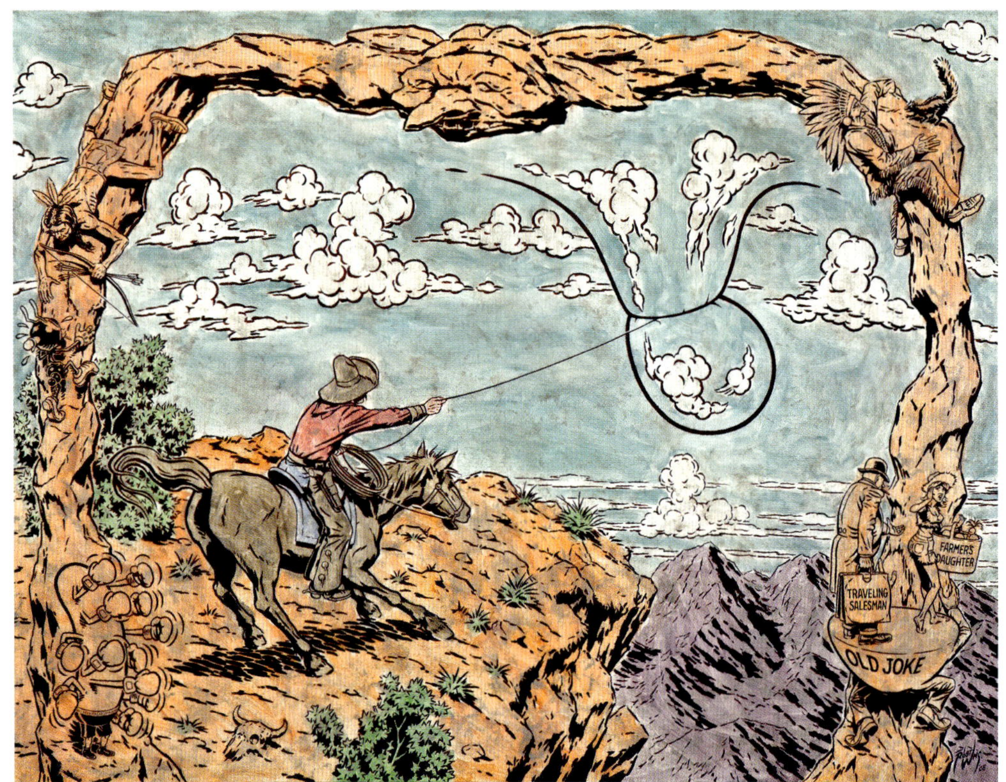

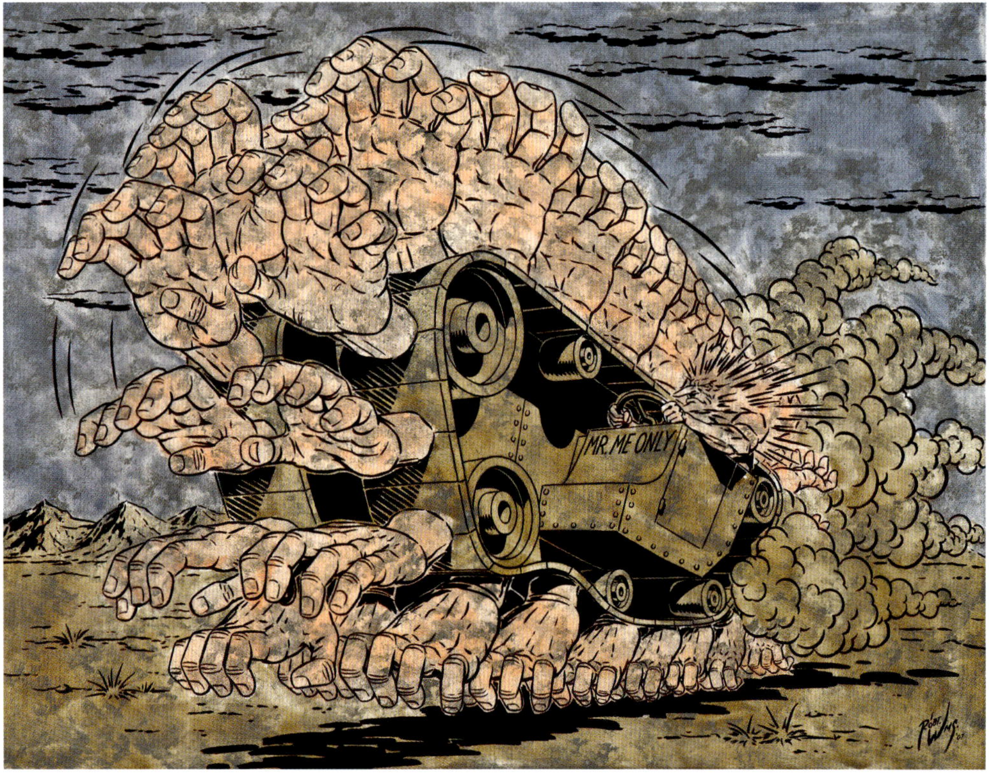

Robert Williams
Wrangling the Firmament, 2008

Robert Williams
Gimme, Gimme, Gimme, 2007

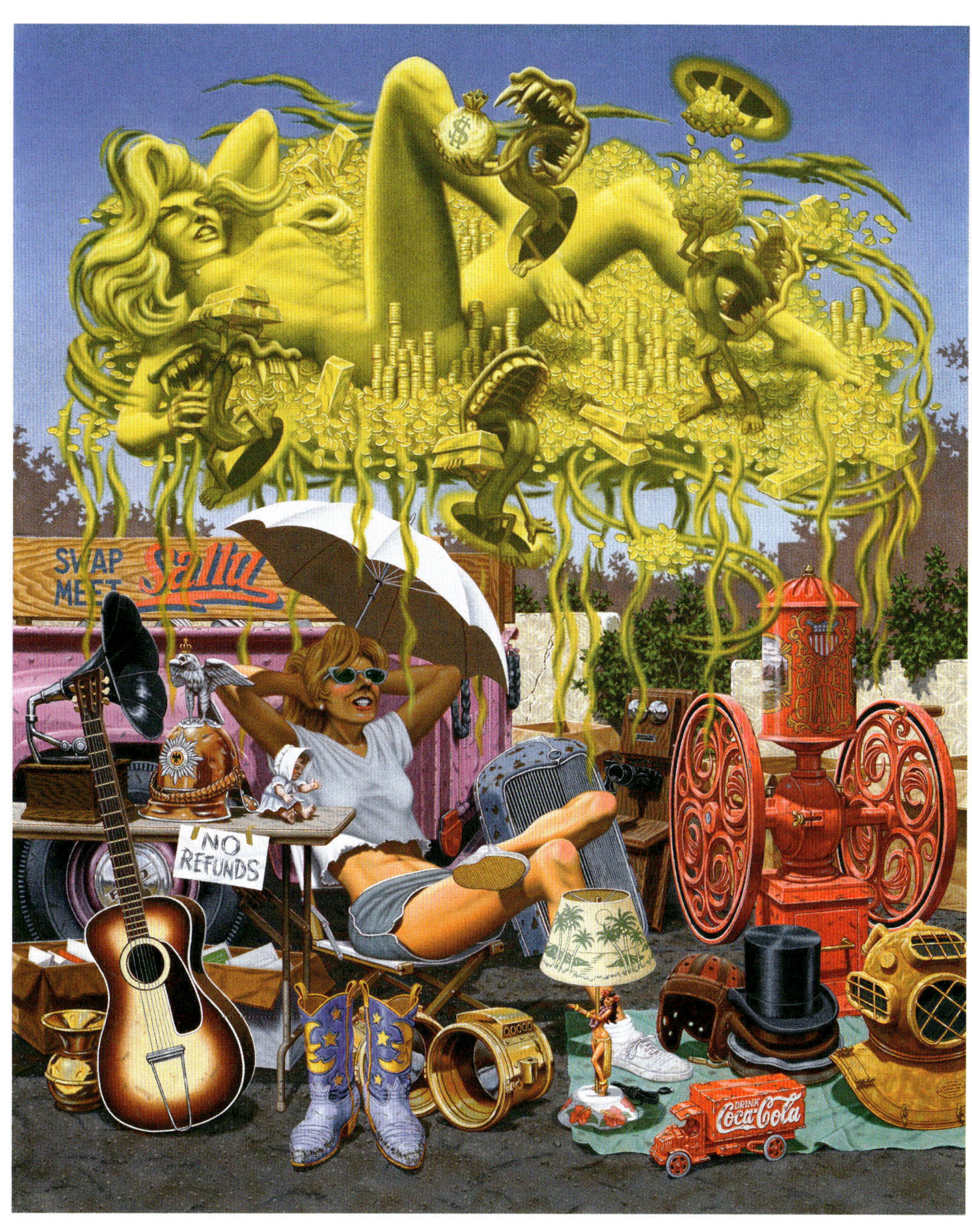

Robert Williams
Swap Meet Sally, 2005

Robert Williams
Creation Trumps Creator, 2010

Ed Moses
Me, 2011

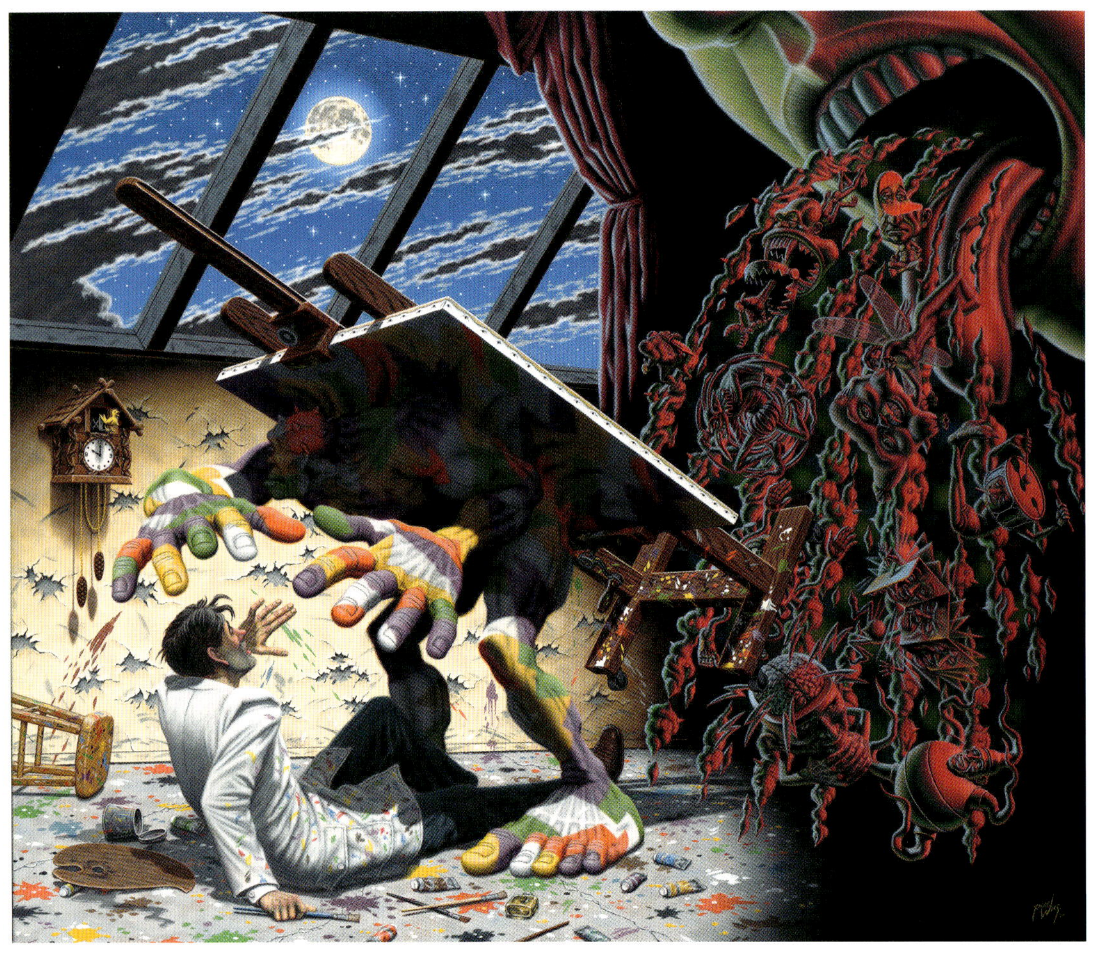

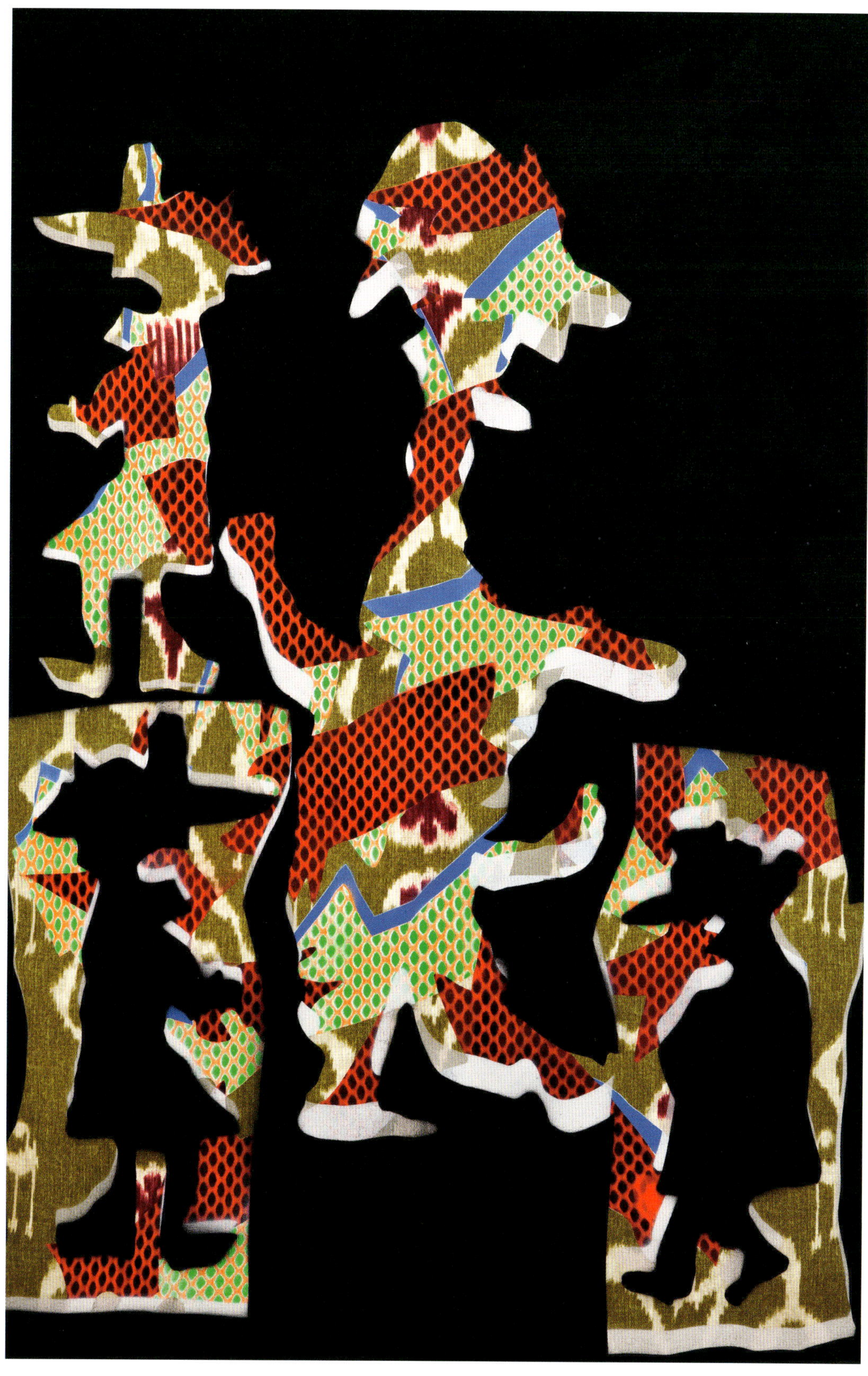

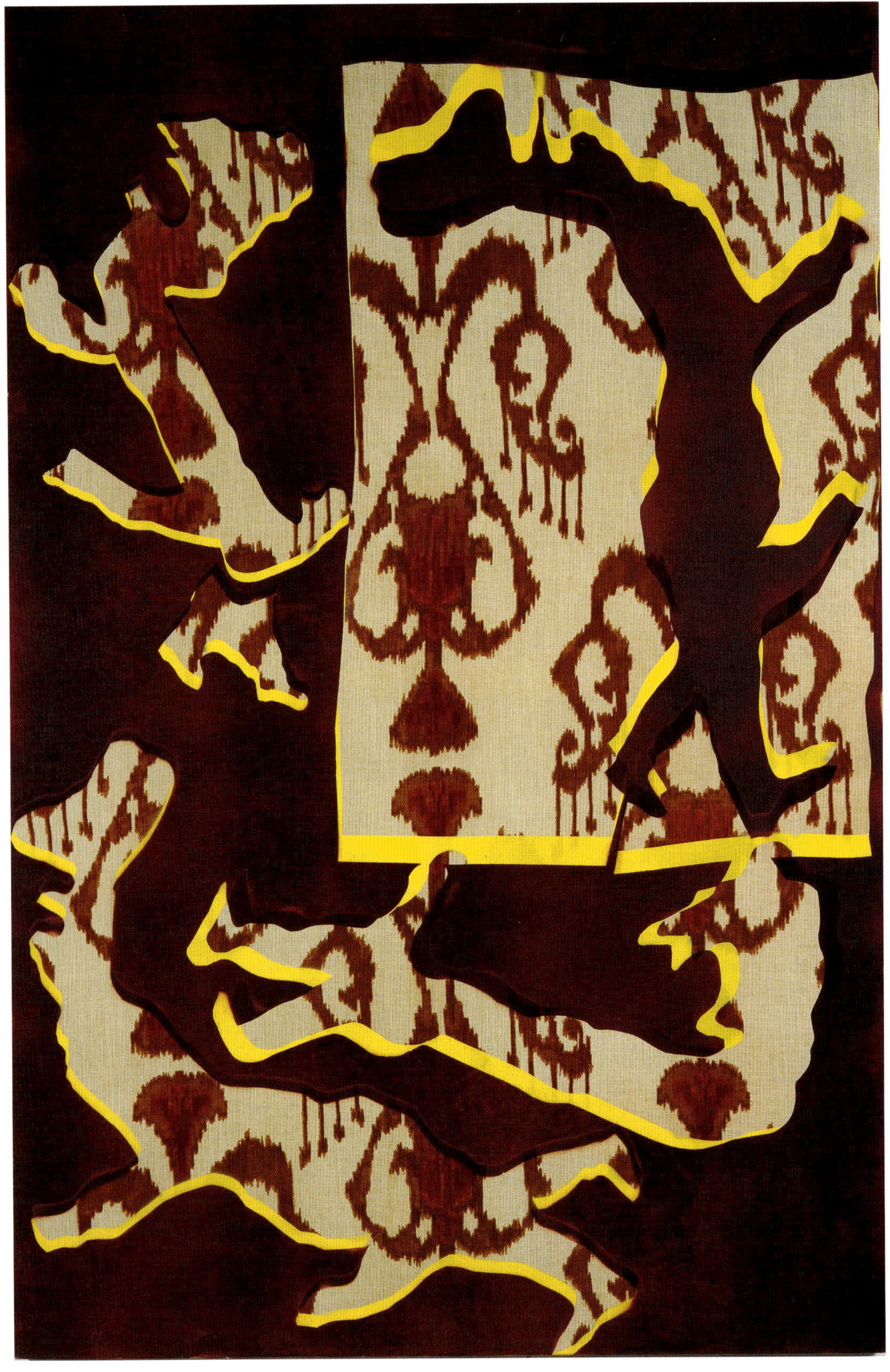

Ed Moses
Hed-Owt #2, 2011

Ed Moses
Hed-Owt #3, 2011

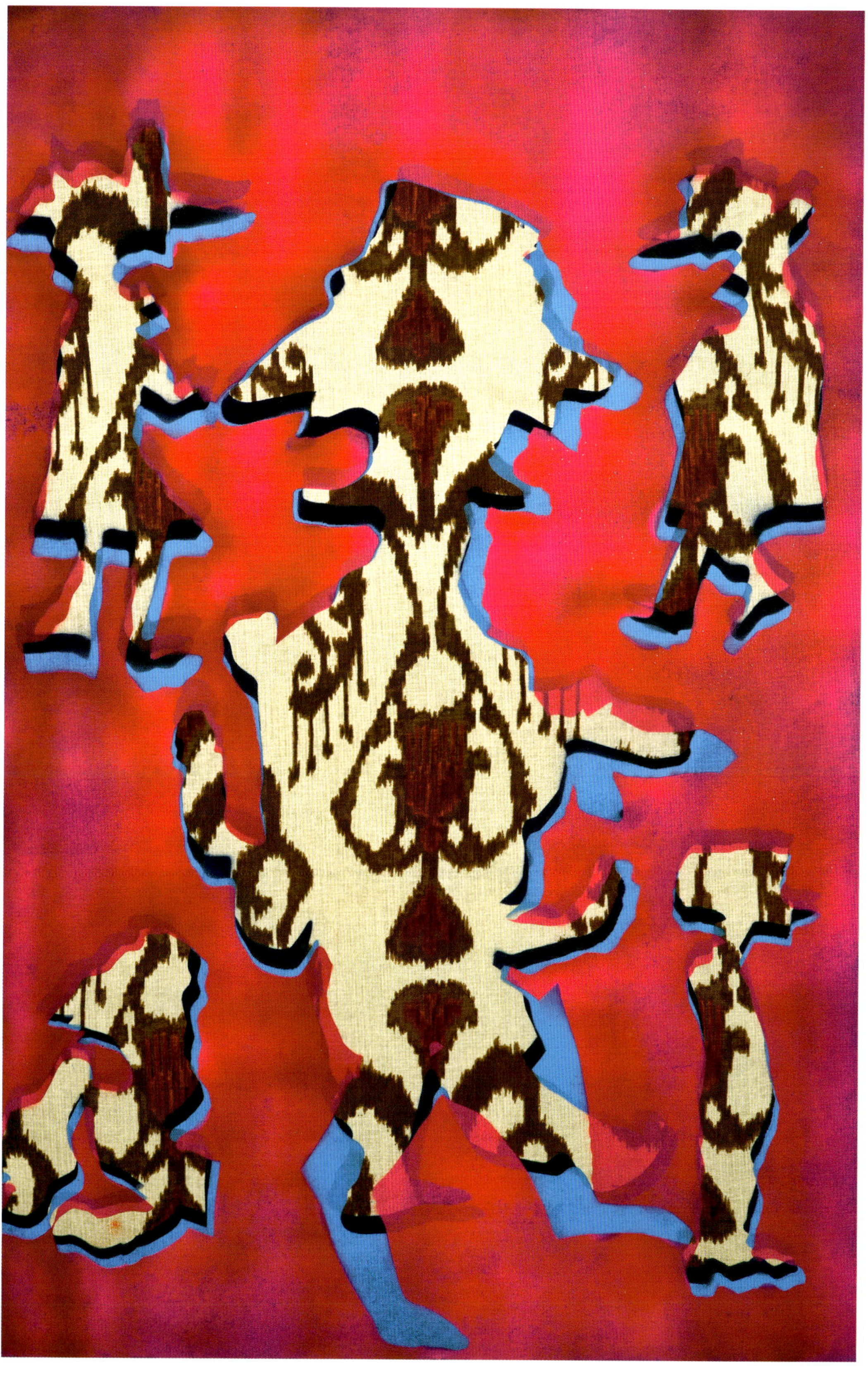

Artists’ Biographies

John Baldessari

John Baldessari's text-and-image paintings from the mid-1960s are widely recognized as among the earliest examples of conceptual art, while his 1980s photo compositions derived from film stills were pivotal to the development of appropriation art and other practices that address the social and cultural impact of mass culture. By using the process of montage to combine language and reorganize imagery, Baldessari illustrates that meaning is constructed relationally rather than through a fixed system of language. His layered, often humorous compositions carry disparate connotations, underscoring how relative and plural meaning is. Pedagogy also plays a major role in his practice. He has taught throughout his career, and the didactic strategies that he deploys in his work—experimentation, rule-based systems, and working within and against arbitrarily imposed limits to find new solutions to problems—are intrinsic to his worldview and philosophy.

Baldessari was born in National City, California, in 1931. He earned degrees at San Diego State University (BFA, 1953; MFA, 1957) and did additional postgraduate work at the University of California, Berkeley (1954–55); the University of California, Los Angeles (1955); Los Angeles County Art Institute (1957–59); and Chouinard Art Institute (1957–59). He taught at the California Institute of the Arts in Valencia from 1970 to 1988 and the University of California, Los Angeles, from 1996 to 2007. His artwork has been featured in more than two hundred solo exhibitions, including the current traveling retrospective *John Baldessari: Pure Beauty* (2009–11), and in more than one thousand group exhibitions in the United States and Europe. Baldessari lives and works in Los Angeles.

Selected Bibliography

2010

- Drohojowska-Philp, Hunter. *John Baldessari: A Print Retrospective from the Collections of Jordan D. Schnitzer and His Family Foundation*. Exh. cat. Portland, OR: Jordan Schnitzer Family Foundation; San Francisco: Fine Arts Museums of San Francisco, 2010.

2009

- Hurowitz, Sharon Coplan. *John Baldessari: A Catalogue Raisonné of Prints and Multiples, 1971–2007*. Manchester, VT: Hudson Hills Press, 2009.
- Morgan, Jessica, and Leslie Jones. *John Baldessari: Pure Beauty*. Exh. cat. Los Angeles: Los Angeles County Museum of Art; New York: DelMonico Books • Prestel, 2009.

2008

- *John Baldessari: BACA Laureate 2008*. Exh. cat. Maastricht, the Netherlands: Bonnefantenmuseum, 2008.

2007

- Gronert, Stefan, and Christina Végh, eds. *John Baldessari: Music*. Exh. cat., Kunstmuseum Bonn and Bonner Kunstverein. Cologne: König, 2007.

2006

- *John Baldessari: The Prima Facie Series*. Exh. cat. Deurle, Belgium: Museum Dhondt-Dhaenens, 2006.

2005

- Brugerolle, Marie de. *John Baldessari: From Life*. Paris: Ecole Normale Supérieure des Beaux-Arts; Nîmes, France: Carré d'Art–Musée d'Art Contemporain, 2005.
- Pakesch, Peter, ed. *John Baldessari: Life's Balance: Werke 84–04 / Works 84–04*. Exh. cat., Kunsthaus Graz. Cologne: König, 2005.

2004

- *John Baldessari: Somewhere between Almost Right and Not Quite (with Orange)*. Exh. cat. Berlin: Deutsche Guggenheim; New York: Guggenheim Museum Publications, 2004.

1999

- Cranston, Meg, et al. *Baldessari: While Something Is Happening Here, Something Else Is Happening There: Works, 1988–1999*. Exh. cat., Sprengel Museum Hannover. Cologne: König, 1999.

1998

- *Baldessari–RMS W VU: Wallpaper, Lamps, and Plants (New)*. Exh. cat., Museum für Gegenwartskunst Zürich. Zurich: Migros, 1998.

1996

- Davies, Hugh, and Andrea Hales, eds. *John Baldessari: National City*. Exh. cat. San Diego: Museum of Contemporary Art, 1996.

1990

- Bruggen, Coosje van. *John Baldessari*. New York: Rizzoli, 1990.

1981

- Tucker, Marcia, et al. *John Baldessari*. Exh. cat. New York: New Museum, 1981.

Sarah Cain

Sarah Cain's practice incorporates works on paper, painting, sculpture, and site-specific installation. Her work is an investigation of the various forms of space: psychic, physical, and emotional. Cain was born in Albany, New York, in 1979 and lives and works in Los Angeles. She studied at San Francisco Art Institute (BFA, 2001); Skowhegan School of Painting and Sculpture (2006); and the University of California, Berkeley (MFA, 2006). She received the 2006 San Francisco Museum of Modern Art SECA Award. She has had solo exhibitions at Santa Barbara Contemporary Arts Forum (2011); Bryan Miller Gallery, Houston (2010); Anne Mosseri-Marlio Galerie, Zurich (2009); Sara Meltzer Gallery, New York (2009, 2010); Art Positions, Art Basel Miami Beach (2009); and Anthony Meier Fine Arts, San Francisco (2009, 2006). She has also participated in group exhibitions at the San Francisco Museum of Modern Art (2011, 2007); the Aspen Art Museum (2007); and the Berkeley Art Museum (2006). Her work was included in the 2006 Busan Biennale, Busan, South Korea, and in the 2008 California Biennial at the Orange County Museum of Art. She created a site-specific installation for *Nothing Beside Remains*, organized by Los Angeles Nomadic Division in Marfa, Texas (2011). Cain has forthcoming solo exhibitions at Honor Fraser, Los Angeles (2012), and Anthony Meier Fine Arts, San Francisco (2013), and her work will appear in *Gold* at the Imperial Belvedere Palace Museum, Vienna (2012).

Selected Bibliography

2011

- Nelson, Steffie. "Space Invader." *T Magazine, New York Times*, September 26, 2011, http://tmagazine.blogs.nytimes.com/2011/09/26/space-invader/?scp=1&sq=sarah%20cain&st=cse.

2010

- Alvarez, Olivia Flores. "Little by Little." *Houston Press*, July 22, 2010.
- Britt, Douglas. "Art Exhibits: Portraits, Psychedelic Pieces Worth Seeing." *Houston Chronicle*, August 13, 2010.

2009

- Cornell, Lauren, et al. *The Younger than Jesus Artist Directory*. Exh. cat., New Museum of Contemporary Art. New York: Phaidon, 2009.

2008

- Hoffmann, Jens. "Sarah Cain: In Conversation with Jens Hoffman." *2008 California Biennial.* Exh. cat. Newport Beach, CA: Orange County Museum of Art, 2008.
- Rosenberg, Karen. "Art in Review: Landscapes for Frankenstein." *New York Times*, August 1, 2008.

2007

- Brenneman, Christine. "Big, Bold, and Bright." *Marin Independent Journal*, January 30, 2007.
- McDowell, Tara. "Sarah Cain." In *2006 SECA Art Award: Sarah Cain, Kota Ezawa, Amy Franceschini, Mitzi Pederson, Leslie Shows.* Exh. cat. San Francisco: San Francisco Museum of Modern Art, 2007.
- Ruiz, Alma. "Juror's Comments." In *New American Paintings: Juried Exhibitions-in-Print; Pacific Coast Number 73.* Boston: Open Studios Press, 2007.
- Zuckerman, Heidi. *Like Color in Pictures.* Exh. cat. Aspen: Aspen Art Museum, 2007.

2006

- Buuck, David. "Sarah Cain at Anthony Meier Fine Arts." *Artweek* 37 (November 2006): 12–13.
- Cash, Stephanie. "Report from San Francisco II: New and Now." *Art in America* 94 (January 2006): 57.
- *A Tale of Two Cities: Busan-Seoul/ Seoul-Busan.* Exh. cat. Busan, S. Korea: Busan Biennale, 2006.

2005

- Schaefer, Carey Ann. *Book of Small.* Vancouver: Canadian Council for the Arts, 2005.

2004

- Knobel, Kyle. "Interview with Sarah Cain." *Record/Play*, April 2004, 8–11.

2003

- Westbrook, Lindsey. "Sarah Cain: New Work." *San Francisco Bay Guardian*, February 5, 2003.

Llyn Foulkes

Llyn Foulkes has lived and worked in Los Angeles for more than fifty years, and the environmental, commercial, and cultural topography of the city continues to be a source of inspiration and reflection for him. His depictions of the landscape convey the nostalgia of prewar utopian ideals of American life. His recent large-scale narrative tableaux merge sculpture with painting, involving a long and methodical process of adding and subtracting elements to create layers of depth and illusion, of oblique and direct iconographies. They have taken as long as seven years to complete.

Music also plays a very important part in Foulkes's life. He played the drums with City Lights (1965–71), then started his own band, called the Rubber Band (1973–77). Since the 1980s Foulkes has performed as a one-man band with a homemade instrument called the Machine. He performs regularly on the West Coast and released a recording of original compositions, *Llyn Foulkes and His Machine: Live at the Church of Art* (2004).

Foulkes was born in Yakima, Washington, in 1934 and attended Chouinard Art Institute from 1957 to 1959. He began showing at the legendary Ferus Gallery, where he had his first one-person show in 1961. Subsequent solo exhibitions have taken place at the Laguna Art Museum, the Santa Barbara Contemporary Arts Forum, the Pasadena Art Museum, and the Oakland Museum. His work has also been featured in group exhibitions at the Museum of Contemporary Art, Chicago; the San Francisco Museum of Modern Art; the Museum of Modern Art and the Whitney Museum of American Art, New York; the Moderna Museet, Stockholm; and the Centre Pompidou, Paris. Foulkes is the subject of a documentary by Tamar Halpern, which is currently in production.

Selected Bibliography

2011

- Curiger, Bice, and Giovanni Carmine, eds. *ILLUMInations: 54. Esposizione internazionale d'arte, la Biennale di Venezia.* Exh. cat. Venice: Fondazione, la Biennale di Venezia, 2011.

2009

- Subotnick, Ali. *Nine Lives: Visionary Artists from L.A.* Exh. cat. Los Angeles: Hammer Museum, 2009.

2008

- Nittve, Lars, with Lena Essling, eds. *Time and Place: Los Angeles, 1957–1968.* Exh. cat. Stockholm: Moderna Museet, 2008.

2006

- Grenier, Catherine. *Los Angeles, 1955–1985: Birth of an Art Capital.* Exh. cat. Paris: Centre Pompidou, 2006.
- Selz, Peter. *Art of Engagement: Visual Politics in California and Beyond.* Berkeley: University of California Press, 2006.
- Whiting, Cécile. *Pop L.A.: Art and the City in the 1960s.* Berkeley: University of California Press, 2006.

2005

- Duncan, Michael, and Kristine McKenna. *Semina Culture: Wallace Berman and His Circle.* Exh. cat. Los Angeles: Santa Monica Museum of Art, 2005.

1999

- Belloli, Jay. *Radical Past: Contemporary Art and Music in Pasadena, 1960–1974.* Exh. cat. Pasadena, CA: Armory Center for the Arts, 1999.

1995

- Knode, Marilu, et al. *Llyn Foulkes: Between a Rock and a Hard Place.* Exh. cat. Laguna Beach, CA: Laguna Art Museum, 1995.

1992

- Schimmel, Paul. *Helter Skelter.* Exh. cat. Los Angeles: Museum of Contemporary Art, 1992.

1989

- Ayres, Anne. *L.A. Pop in the Sixties.* Newport Beach, CA: Newport Harbor Art Museum, 1989.
- *Forty Years of California Assemblage.* Exh. cat. Los Angeles: Wight Art Gallery, University of California, 1989.

1986

- Hopper, Dennis. *Out of the Sixties.* Pasadena, CA: Twelvetrees Press, 1986.
- Siff, Elena. *Southern California Assemblage: Past and Present.* Santa Barbara: Santa Barbara Contemporary Arts Forum and College of Creative Studies Gallery, University of California, 1986.

1974

- *Llyn Foulkes: Fifty Paintings, Collages, and Prints from Southern California Collections: A Survey Exhibition, 1959–1974.* Newport Beach, CA: Newport Harbor Art Museum, 1974.

George Herms

A seminal figure in the development of West Coast assemblage beginning in the late 1950s, George Herms continues to amass discarded objects salvaged from quotidian life and found materials intercepted from popular culture with steadfast patience and affectionate stamina. His alchemy transforms detritus into new objects of love and beauty. His assemblage aesthetic extends to a wide range of disciplines, including painting, sculpture, drawing, collage, performance, photography, and filmmaking. Influenced by the Beat generation, Herms also infuses elements of music–specifically jazz–and poetry into his work.

Herms was born in Woodland, California, in 1935 and studied at the University of California, Berkeley, in 1955. Recent projects include a solo show at the Museum of Contemporary Art, Los Angeles, and a jazz opera, which debuted at REDCAT in February 2011. His works have been prominently featured at several California institutions, including the Santa Monica Museum of Art, Santa Monica; the Crocker Art Museum, Sacramento; the Riverside Art Museum, Riverside; and the Newport Harbor Art Museum, Newport Beach. Herms lives and works in Southern California.

Selected Bibliography

2006
- Grenier, Catherine. *Los Angeles, 1955–1985: Birth of an Art Capital.* Exh. cat. Paris: Centre Pompidou, 2006.

2005
- *George Herms: Hot Set.* Exh. cat. Santa Monica, California: Santa Monica Museum of Art, 2005. Booklet and DVD.

2003
- *George Herms, Then and Now: Fifty Years of Assemblage.* Exh. cat. Philadelphia: Seraphin Gallery; New York: ACA Galleries, 2003.

1992
- *George Herms: The Secret Archives.* Exh. cat. Los Angeles: Los Angeles Municipal Art Gallery, 1992.

1990
- Solnit, Rebecca. *Secret Exhibition: Six California Artists of the Cold War Era.* San Francisco: City Lights, 1990.

1989
- *Forty Years of California Assemblage.* Exh. cat. Los Angeles: Wight Art Gallery, University of California, 1989.

1984
- Garver, Thomas H. *George Herms: Rome Poem.* Exh. cat. Fullerton: Art Gallery, California State University, 1984.

1979
- Turnbull, Betty. *The Prometheus Archives: A Retrospective Exhibition of the Works of George Herms.* Newport Beach, CA: Newport Harbor Art Museum, 1979.

1968
- Glicksman, Hal. *Assemblage in California: Works from the Late 50s and Early 60s.* Exh. cat. Irvine: Art Gallery, University of California, 1968.

1961
- Seitz, William. *Art of Assemblage.* Exh. cat. New York: Museum of Modern Art, 1961.

Stanya Kahn

Stanya Kahn is a Los Angeles–based video artist whose practice includes performance, writing, and sound design. She has exhibited collaboratively with artist Harry Dodge in the last decade and has exhibited solo since 2010. Prior to her collaboration with Dodge, she made solo performance works and toured live shows worldwide from 1992 to 2000. Kahn's hybrid media practice combines storytelling with visceral performances and is infused with pop vernacular, documentary tropes, improvisation, and experimental film/video praxis, inhabiting a space between fiction and document.

Kahn was born in San Francisco in 1968 and received degrees from San Francisco State University (BA, 1991) and Bard College (MFA, 2003). Her work has been shown at the Museum of Contemporary Art, the Getty Center, and the Hammer Museum in Los Angeles; the Fifty-Fourth Venice Biennale Film Program at the Swiss Pavilion; the Sundance Film Festival, Park City, Utah; ZKM / Center for Art and Media, Karlsruhe, Germany; the Museum of Modern Art, New York; P.S. 1 Contemporary Art Center, Long Island City, New York; Susanne Vielmetter Los Angeles Projects; and Elizabeth Dee Gallery, New York. She also participated in the 2008 Whitney Biennial in New York and the 2010 California Biennial at the Orange County Museum of Art. She has received grants from the California Community Foundation, the Durfee Foundation, and the Fund for US Artists at International Festivals and Exhibitions, among others. She teaches at the University of California, Los Angeles; California Institute of the Arts, Valencia; and Otis College of Art and Design, Los Angeles.

Selected Bibliography

2011
- Knight, Christopher. "It's a Trek Worth Exploring." *Los Angeles Times*, January 7, 2011.

2010
- Campagnola, Sonia. "Stanya Kahn at Susanne Vielmetter Los Angeles Projects." *Flash Art*, no. 272 (May–June 2010): 115.
- Kramer, David Jacob. "Stanya Kahn, a Video Artist Who Defies Characterization." *Papermag*, October 30, 2010, http://www.papermag.com/arts_and_style/2010/10/stanya-kahn.php.

- Wahlquist, Grant. "Stanya Kahn: Interview." In *2010 California Biennial*. Exh. cat. Newport Beach, CA: Orange County Museum of Art; Munich: DelMonico Books/Prestel, 2008.

2009
- Elben, Georg, ed. *Videonale 12*. Exh. cat. Cologne: Dumont, 2009.
- Smith, Michael. "Harry Dodge and Stanya Kahn." *Bomb Magazine*, no. 108 (Summer 2009), http://bombsite.com/issues/108/articles/3302.

2008
- Bedford, Christopher. "Focus: Harry Dodge and Stanya Kahn." *Frieze*, no. 119 (November–December 2008), http://www.frieze.com/issue/article/harry_dodge_and_stanya_kahn/.
- Finkel, Jori. "Unsettling, in a Funny Sort of Way." *New York Times*, March 2, 2008.
- Huldisch, Henriette, and Shamim M. Momin, eds. *Whitney Biennial 2008*. Exh. cat. New York: Whitney Museum of American Art, 2008.
- Kataoka, Mami. *Laughing in a Foreign Language*. Exh. cat. London: Hayward Gallery, 2008.
- Kushner, Rachel. "1,000 Words: Harry Dodge and Stanya Kahn." *Artforum* 46 (January 2008): 240–43.
- Phillips, Glenn, ed. *California Video: Artists and Histories*. Exh. cat. Los Angeles: Getty Publications, 2008.

2007
- Blumenstein, Ellen, and Felix Ensslin, eds. *Between Two Deaths*. Exh. cat., ZKM / Center for Art and Media. Ostfildern, Germany: Hatje Cantz, 2007.
- Garrels, Gary. *Eden's Edge*. Exh. cat. Los Angeles: Hammer Museum, 2007.

2006
- Smith, Roberta. "Art in Review: Harry Dodge and Stanya Kahn." *New York Times*, May 12, 2006.

2005
- Johnson, Ken. "Stanya Kahn and Harriet (Harry) Dodge." *New York Times*, August 5, 2005.

2000
- Covan, Ellie. "Politics, Nakedness, and Other Hot Topics." *New York Times*, September 20, 2000.

1998
- Dunning, Jennifer. "Fallen Angels in Energetic Theatricality." *New York Times*, December 12, 1998.

Shana Lutker

Drawing from the archives of psychoanalysis and surrealism, Shana Lutker's work asks questions about the way experience and interpretation inflect and infect history and objects. Her bodies of work function as uncanny "case studies" of subjects, as encountered by the artist in archives and on the Internet. Installations often combine photographs, drawings, found objects, and sculpture.

Lutker was born in Northport, New York, in 1978 and is a graduate of Brown University (BA, 2000) and the University of California, Los Angeles (MFA, 2005). She has had solo exhibitions at Barbara Seiler Galerie, Zurich; Susanne Vielmetter Los Angeles Projects; Artists Space, New York; CCA Wattis Institute for Contemporary Arts, San Francisco; and Wetterling Gallery, Stockholm. She has participated in group exhibitions at the Massachusetts Museum of Contemporary Art, North Adams; D'Amelio Terras and Harris Lieberman, New York; and Luckman Gallery and Honor Fraser, Los Angeles. Her work was featured in the 2006 and 2008 California Biennials at the Orange County Museum of Art and in Performa 09 in New York. Lutker is managing editor of *X-TRA* and lives and works in Los Angeles.

Selected Bibliography

2011
- Latimer, Quinn. "Shana Lutker." *Frieze*, no. 141 (September 2011), http://www.frieze.com/issue/review/shana-lutker/.

2010
- Wu, Cassie. "Shana Lutker." Artforum.com, June 2010, http://artforum.com/picks/id=25989&view=print.

2009
- Ennis, Ciara. *Veronica: Rheim Alkadhi, Nadine Hottenrott, Karen Lofgren, Shana Lutker, Mathilde ter Heijne, Jeni Spota, Joy Whalen, Carrie Yury*. Claremont, CA: Pitzer Art Galleries, Pitzer College, 2009.
- Haeg, Fritz. *The Sundown Salon Unfolding Archive*. New York: Evil Twin Books, 2009.
- Cornell, Lauren, et al. *The Younger than Jesus Artist Directory*. Exh. cat., New Museum of Contemporary Art. New York: Phaidon, 2009.
- Myers, Holly. "Attitude and Talent to Spare." *Los Angeles Times*, August 21, 2009.

2008
- Firstenberg, Lauri. "Shana Lutker: In Conversation with Lauri Firstenberg." In *2008 California Biennial*. Exh. cat. Newport Beach, CA: Orange County Museum of Art, 2008.
- Foss, Paul. "Shana Lutker." *ArtUS*, no. 23 (Summer 2008): 7.
- Frank, Peter. "The Radiant Mind, the Body Politic: Lee Mullican, Shana Lutker, and Olga Koumoundouros." *LA Weekly*, June 4, 2008, http://www.laweekly.com/2008-06-05/art-books/the-radiant-mind-the-body-politic/.
- Mizota, Sharon. "Eureka Moments." *Los Angeles Times*, October 19, 2008.
- Uslip, Jeffrey. *Shana Lutker: Combined Faulty Acts*. New York: Artists Space, 2008.

2007
- Beil, Kim. "California Biennial at OCMA." *Artweek* 38 (February 2007): 16–19.
- Carson, Juli. *Shana Lutker's "The Future of an Illusion."* Exh. brochure. Irvine: Room Gallery, University of California, 2007.
- Hoffmann, Jens. "Fragments of an Analysis of a Case of Art." In *Shana Lutker: Passengers 1.4*. Exh. brochure. San Francisco: CCA Wattis Institute for Contemporary Arts, 2007.

2006
- Holte, Michael Ned. "Shana Lutker." In *2006 California Biennial*. Newport Beach, CA: Orange County Museum of Art, 2006.
- Myers, Julian. "I Want to Tell You Everything." In *Shana Lutker: "Excerpts."* Exh. cat. Stockholm: Wetterling Gallery, 2006.

Ed Moses

Ed Moses has been a central figure in the Los Angeles art scene since the late 1950s, having had his first solo show at the legendary Ferus Gallery in 1958. In a career that has spanned more than fifty years, his painting practice—influenced by distinctly American art movements such as abstract expressionism, pop art, hard edge, color field, and minimalism—has sustained a consistent discipline and methodology while simultaneously resisting a monolithic signature style. His oeuvre includes compositions featuring repeated decorative patterns as well as hard-edge geometric designs. His pluralistic approach indicates a commitment to avoiding stylistic limitations. For Moses, painting is a visceral experience, and his paintings are metaphors for his existence on earth. The process of mark making, in which each repetitive stroke is a moment open to spontaneity and chance, also serves as evidence of the artist's hand.

Moses was born in Long Beach, California, in 1926 and received degrees at the University of California, Los Angeles (BA, 1955; MA, 1958). In 1996 the Museum of Contemporary Art, Los Angeles, organized a retrospective of his paintings and drawings. Other solo shows have taken place at the Los Angeles County Museum of Art and Pomona College Art Gallery in Claremont, California. In addition to showing at Ferus Gallery, Moses has exhibited his work at other renowned Los Angeles galleries, including Riko Mizuno Gallery, Margo Leavin Gallery, and L.A. Louver. His work has been exhibited at the Norton Simon Museum and the Armory Center for the Arts in Pasadena, California; the Hammer Museum, Los Angeles; and the Newport Harbor Art Museum, Newport Beach, California. He participated in the 1990 Whitney Biennial in New York and received a Guggenheim Fellowship in 1980. Moses lives and works in Venice, California.

Selected Bibliography

2010

- Moses, Ed. *Ed Moses: Drawings of the Sixties*. Exh. cat. Los Angeles: Ferus Gallery, 2010.

2009

- Haskell, Barbara, et al. *Ed Moses*. Santa Fe, NM: Radius, 2009.

2005

- *Ed Moses: Paintings*. Exh. cat. Mill Valley, CA: Robert Green Fine Arts, 2005.

1999

- Colpitt, Frances. *Ed Moses*. Exh. cat. Venice, CA: L.A. Louver, 1999.

1996

- Yau, John. *Ed Moses: A Retrospective of the Paintings and Drawings, 1951–1996*. Exh. cat. Los Angeles: Museum of Contemporary Art, 1996.

1989

- Afif, Steve. *Ed Moses: New Graphics, 1988–89*. Exh. cat. New York: Galeria Joan Prats, 1989.
- *Ed Moses*. Exh. cat. Seoul: Kukje Gallery, 1989.

1986

- Linker, Kate, et al. *Individuals: A Selected History of Contemporary Art, 1945–1986*. Exh. cat. Los Angeles: Museum of Contemporary Art, 1986.

1981

- *Southern California Artists, 1940–1981*. Exh. cat. Laguna Beach, CA: Laguna Beach Museum of Art, 1981.
- Tuchman, Maurice. *Los Angeles: Seventeen Artists in the Sixties*. Exh. cat. Los Angeles: Los Angeles County Museum of Art, 1981.

1976

- Barron, Stephanie. *Ed Moses: New Paintings*. Exh. cat. Los Angeles: Los Angeles County Museum of Art, 1976.
- Masheck, Joseph. *Ed Moses: Drawings, 1958–1976*. Exh. cat. Los Angeles: Frederick W. Wight Art Gallery, University of California, 1976.
- Turnbull, Betty. *The Last Time I Saw Ferus, 1957–1966*. Exh. cat. Newport Beach, CA: Newport Harbor Art Museum, 1976.

1971

- *Thirty-Second Biennial Exhibition of Contemporary American Painting*. Exh. cat. Washington, DC: Corcoran Gallery of Art, 1971.

1969

- Coplans, John, ed. *West Coast, 1945–1969*. Exh. cat. Pasadena, CA: Pasadena Art Museum, 1969.

1967

- Monte, James. *Late Fifties at the Ferus*. Exh. cat. Los Angeles: Los Angeles County Museum of Art, 1967.

1962

- Goodrich, Lloyd, and George Culler. *Fifty California Artists*. Exh. cat. San Francisco: San Francisco Museum of Art, 1962.

Amanda Ross-Ho

Amanda Ross-Ho is a mixed-media artist who often incorporates found objects into paintings, drawings, sculptures, installations, and photographs. Her method of assemblage employs images and media from myriad cultural locations, along with found objects that contain personal and historical references. Intermixing and displacing these disparate objects, Ross-Ho presents an intersection where meaning is deciphered beyond the singularity of vision into the multidimensional, requiring peripheral awareness, temporal consideration, and the activation of memory and association.

Ross-Ho was born in Chicago in 1975 and is a graduate of the School of the Art Institute of Chicago (BFA, 1998) and the University of Southern California (MFA, 2006). She has had solo exhibitions at the Pomona College Museum of Art, Claremont, California; Cherry and Martin, Los Angeles; Mitchell-Innes and Nash, New York; the Visual Arts Center, Austin, Texas; and the Approach, London. Her work has been featured in exhibitions at the Museum of Modern Art, New York; Henry Art Gallery, Seattle; the Museum of Contemporary Art, Los Angeles; Artists Space, New York; the Museum of Contemporary Art, Chicago; the New Museum, New York; and the Los Angeles County Museum of Art. She also participated in the 2008 Whitney Biennial in New York and the 2008 California Biennial at the Orange County Museum of Art. Ross-Ho lives and works in Los Angeles.

Selected Bibliography

2011

- Berardini, Andrew. "Amanda Ross-Ho." *Frieze*, no. 137 (March 2011): 116–17.
- Griffin, Jonathan. "Amanda Ross-Ho: A Stack of Black Pants." *Art Review*, no. 47 (January–February): 119.

2010

- Harvey, Doug. "Amanda Ross-Ho: Trick-and-Treater." *L.A. Weekly*, May 20, 2010, http://www.laweekly.com/2010-05-20/la-life/amanda-ross-ho-trick-and-treater/.
- Myers, Holly. "In The Studio: A Playful Stage for Amanda Ross-Ho." *Los Angeles Times*, August 22, 2010.
- Rosenberg, Karen. "Ignoring Boundaries and Borrowing Freely." *New York Times*, October 7, 2010.
- Schjeldahl, Peter. "Amanda Ross-Ho." *New*

Yorker, April 26, 2010, 12–13.
- Stillman, Steel. "In the Studio: Amanda Ross-Ho." *Art in America* 98 (April 2010): 82–89.
- Taft, Catherine. "Amanda Ross-Ho." *Artforum* 46 (April 2010): 204–5.
- Truong, Hong-An. "Absence and Presence in Amanda Ross-Ho's *Somebody Stop Me*." *Idiom*, April 14, 2010, http://idiommag.com/2010/04/absence-and-presence-in-amanda-ross-hos-somebody-stop-me/.
- Wehr, Anne. "Amanda Ross-Ho." *Frieze*, no. 132 (June–August 2010): 185.

2009
- White, Charlie. "Cut and Paste." *Artforum* 47 (March 2009): 210–15.

2008
- Alemani, Cecilia. "Whitney Girls." *Mousse Magazine*, no. 13 (March 2008): 110–12.
- Allan, Stacey. "Introducing Amanda Ross-Ho." *Modern Painters* 20 (March 2008): 46–48, 95.
- Gaines, Malik. "Amanda Ross-Ho: In Conversation with Malik Gaines." In *2008 California Biennial*. Newport Beach, CA: Orange County Museum of Art, 2008.
- Harvey, Doug. "Free Skating." *L.A. Weekly*, September 26–October 2, 2008, 58.
- Mizota, Sharon. "Follow the Clues and, Aha!" *Los Angeles Times*, October 10, 2008.
- Smith, Roberta. "Amanda Ross-Ho and Kirsten Stoltmann." *New York Times*, February 15, 2008.

2007
- Buckley, Annie. "Amanda Ross-Ho at Cherry and Martin." *Artweek* 38 (May 2007): 18.
- Dambrot, Shana Nys. "Amanda Ross-Ho: Nothin Fuckin Matters." *Art Review*, no. 10 (April 2007): 144.
- Holte, Michael Ned. "First Takes: Ten Writers on Up-and-Coming Artists." *Artforum* 45 (January 2007): 208–9.
- Taft, Catherine. "Amanda Ross-Ho." *Modern Painters* 19 (May 2007): 98.
- Vogel, Carol. "Whitney Biennial Stretches to Armory." *New York Times*, November 16, 2007.

2006
- Gray, Emma. "Kitchen Sync." *Art Review* 57 (June 2006): 20–21.
- Smith, Roberta. "Dice Thrown (Will Never Annul Chance)." *New York Times*, November 3, 2006.

Allen Ruppersberg

Allen Ruppersberg constructs new narratives from discarded or forgotten items that have associations with history, literature, popular culture, and everyday life, using various mediums, including sculpture, drawing, painting, photography, collage, video, installation, and text-based objects. He is part of the generation of American conceptualists who pioneered the use of language as art form during the late 1960s and early 1970s. Books and printed ephemera play an especially prominent role in his object-making and storytelling processes. For Ruppersberg the acts of reading and remembering are one and the same; collected ideas are activated and memory associations are in play when we construct and reinvent ideas, which are but reiterations of history. Also known for relocating art display from private institutions to public spaces, Ruppersberg created a number of unforgettable in situ performance installations, most notably *Al's Café* (1969) and *Al's Grand Hotel* (1971) in Los Angeles.

Ruppersberg was born in Cleveland in 1944 and studied at Chouinard Art Institute (BFA, 1967). His first solo exhibition, in 1968, was also the inaugural exhibition of the famed Eugenia Butler Gallery in Los Angeles. Since then, his work has been the subject of more than sixty solo exhibitions, including a major retrospective at the Museum of Contemporary Art, Los Angeles, in 1985, which subsequently traveled to the New Museum of Contemporary Art in New York. His work has been featured in nearly two hundred group shows, and he has participated in the Whitney Biennials in New York (1970, 1975, 1991); Documenta V, Kassel, Germany (1972); and Skulptur Projekte, Münster, Germany (1997). Ruppersberg lives and works in New York and Los Angeles.

Selected Bibliography

2009
- Lewallen, Constance, ed. *Allen Ruppersberg: You and Me or the Art of Give and Take*. Exh. cat., Santa Monica Museum of Art. Zurich: JRP/Ringer, 2009.

2005
- Groos, Ulrike, et al. *Allen Ruppersberg: One of Many–Origins and Variants*. Exh. cat. Düsseldorf: Kunsthalle Düsseldorf; Cologne: König, 2005.

1999
- McCollum, Allan, and Frédéric Paul. *Allen Ruppersberg: Books, Inc.* Exh. cat. Limoges, France: FRAC Limousin, 1999.

1997
- Nittve, Lars, and Helle Crenzien. *Sunshine and Noir: Art in L.A., 1960–1997*. Exh. cat. Humlebaek, Denmark: Louisiana Museum of Modern Art, 1997.

1996
- Aupetitallot, Yves. *Allen Ruppersberg: Where's Al?* Grenoble, France: Centre National d'Art Contemporain, 1996.

1992
- Weelden, Dirk van. *Allen Ruppersberg: A Different Kind of Never-Never-Land*. Exh. cat. Amsterdam: De Appel Foundation, 1992.

1988
- Leonard Starr, Sandra. *Lost and Found in California: Four Decades of Assemblage Art*. Exh. cat. Santa Monica, CA: James Corcoran Gallery, 1988.

1985
- Singerman, Howard. *The Secret of Life and Death: Allen Ruppersberg*. Exh. cat. Los Angeles: Museum of Contemporary Art; Santa Barbara, CA: Black Sparrow Press, 1985.

1981
- Rifkin, Ned. *Stay Tuned*. Exh. cat. New York: New Museum of Contemporary Art, 1981.
- Schimmel, Paul. *Shift: L.A./N.Y.* Exh. cat. Newport Beach, CA: Newport Harbor Art Museum, 1981.

1979
- Speyer, A. James, and Anne Rorimer. *Seventy-Third American Exhibition*. Exh. cat. Chicago: Art Institute of Chicago, 1979.

1977
- Shearer, Linda. *Nine Artists: Theodoron Awards*. Exh. cat. New York: Solomon R. Guggenheim Museum, 1977.

1973
- *Allen Ruppersberg*. Exh. cat. Amsterdam: Stedelijk Museum, 1973.

1972
- Szeemann, Harald. *Documenta V*. Exh. cat. Kassel, Germany: Museum Fridericianum, 1972.
- Winer, Helene. *Allen Ruppersberg*. Exh. cat. Claremont, CA: Pomona College Art Gallery, Montgomery Art Center, 1972.

Robert Williams

Robert Williams is a cartoonist and painter. He contributed to Zap Comix, the seminal underground comics series introduced in the late 1960s, and was also a key figure in Kustom Kulture, an aesthetic subculture linked to hot-rodding and custom cars. In a riposte to the fine art conventions established by the New York art scene, Williams introduced the term *lowbrow art* into the fine arts lexicon in 1979 with the publication of *Lowbrow Art of Robt. Williams*. In 1994 he founded *Juxtapoz Art and Culture Magazine*, devoted to alternative and underground contemporary art. His mix of California car culture, cinematic apocalypticism, pop surrealism, and film noir helped pave the way for a new genre of psychedelic imagery, which he describes as conceptual realism.

Williams was born in 1943 in Albuquerque, New Mexico, and attended Los Angeles City College (1963–64) and Chouinard Art Institute (1965) in Los Angeles. His work has been shown at the Oakland Museum of California; the Institute of Contemporary Art, Boston; the Contemporary Arts Center, Cincinnati; San Francisco Art Institute; the Center of Contemporary Art, Seattle; the Laguna Art Museum, Laguna Beach, California; and the Museum of Contemporary Art, Los Angeles. His large-scale sculptures were exhibited for the first time in *Robert Williams: Conceptual Realism; In the Service of the Hypothetical*, which opened at the Tony Shafrazi Gallery in New York in 2009. In 2010 the documentary film *Robert Williams: Mr. Bitchin'* premiered at the Los Angeles County Museum of Art, with additional screenings at the Museum of Contemporary Art, Los Angeles, and the Museum of Modern Art, New York. Williams's watercolors were shown in the Whitney Biennial (2010), and he also participated in the Lyon Biennale, Lyon, France (2011).

Selected Bibliography

2009
- Williams, Robert. "A Portrait of the Artist as a Young Hot Rodder." In *The All-American Hot Rod: The Cars, the Legends, the Passion*, ed. Michael Dregni, 165–68. Minneapolis: MBI Publishing and Motorbooks, 2009.
- Williams, Robert, and Don Ed Hardy. *Conceptual Realism: In the Service of the Hypothetical*. Seattle: Fantagraphics Books, 2009.

2008
- Beinart, Jon, ed. *Metamorphosis 2: Fifty Contemporary Surreal and Visionary Artists*. Brunswick, Australia: beinArt, 2008.

2006
- Williams, Robert, and Mike LaVella. *The Hot Rod World of Robt. Williams*. Minneapolis: MBI Publishing and Motorbooks, 2006.

2005
- Williams, Robert, and Meg Linton. *Through Prehensile Eyes: Seeing the Art of Robert Williams*. Exh. cat., Maltz Gallery. San Francisco: Last Gasp, 2005.

2004
- Anderson, Kirsten, ed. *Pop Surrealism: The Rise of Underground Art*. San Francisco: Ignition Publishing and Last Gasp, 2004.

2002
- Williams, Robert. *Hysteria in Remission*. Seattle: Fantagraphics Books, 2002.

1997
- Williams, Robert, and Walter Hopps. *Malicious Resplendence*. Seattle: Fantagraphics Books, 1997.

1995
- McCormick, Carlo. "Cartoon Surrealism: An Interview with Robert Williams." *Grand Street*, no. 52 (Spring 1995): 47–57.

1993
- Williams, Robert, and Dr. Timothy Leary. *Views from a Tortured Libido*. San Francisco: Last Gasp, 1993.

1992
- Schimmel, Paul. *Helter Skelter: L.A. Art in the 1990s*. Exh. cat. Los Angeles: Museum of Contemporary Art, 1992.

1989
- Williams, Robert, and Lydia Lynch. *Visual Addiction: The Art of Robert Williams*. San Francisco: Last Gasp, 1989.

1986
- Williams, Robert, and Robert Crumb. *Zombie Mystery Paintings*. San Francisco: Last Gasp, 1986.

1979
- Williams, Robert. *Lowbrow Art of Robt. Williams*. San Francisco: Rip Off Press, 1979.

Works in the Exhibition

Sarah Cain and George Herms

***Korral*, 2011**
Mixed-media room installation
Dimensions variable

Includes the following works:

On walls (left to right):
Sarah Cain
***Untitled (Fall 2011)*, 2011**
Oil pastel, acrylic, beads, thread, and wire on canvas; acrylic on wall and floor
104 1/4 x 88 x 83 1/2 in.
(264.8 x 223.5 x 212.1 cm)
Courtesy of the artist; Anthony Meier Fine Arts, San Francisco; and Honor Fraser Gallery, Los Angeles

Sarah Cain
***Untitled (Strings)*, 2010**
Acrylic and gouache on sheet music
22 1/16 x 17 3/4 in. (56 x 45 cm)
Collection of Abby and Andreas Beroutsos

Sarah Cain
***French Braid*, 2011**
Oil pastel, acrylic, and pencil on canvas
60 x 48 x 4 in. (152.4 x 121.9 x 10.2 cm)
Courtesy of the artist; Honor Fraser Gallery, Los Angeles; and Anthony Meier Fine Arts, San Francisco

George Herms
Duncan McNaughton's book *Capricci* (Bolinas, CA: Blue Millennium Press, 2003), opened to the poem "Me and Mrs. Jones"
Book
Courtesy of the artist

George Herms
***Me and Mrs. Jones*, 2011**
Assemblage
15 x 23 7/8 x 3 1/4 in. (38.1 x 60.6 x 8.3 cm)
Courtesy of the artist

Sarah Cain
***Untitled (Spring 2011)*, 2011**
Sand, acrylic, gold, silver and bronze leaf, thread, Beva, and Holifax on canvas and Masonite
108 1/4 x 81 3/8 x 12 in.
(275 x 206.7 x 30.5 cm)
Courtesy of the artist; Honor Fraser Gallery, Los Angeles; and Anthony Meier Fine Arts, San Francisco

George Herms
***Seitz*, 2011**
Assemblage
Approx. 20 1/2 x 18 5/8 x 10 1/2 in.
(52.1 x 47.3 x 26.7 cm)
Courtesy of the artist

Sarah Cain and George Herms
***From a letter sent by Bill Seitz in the early 50s to Marion Willard, his art dealer in New York…*, 2011**
Excerpted text and description, printed on paper with handwritten note from George Herms to Sarah Cain in ink and highlighter
White copy paper, framed
8 1/2 x 11 in. (21.6 x 27.9 cm)
Courtesy of the artists

On floor (display cases):
George Herms
***Dos Quesadillas*, 2011**
2 display cases with mini sculpture installations
Dimensions variable (each case approx. 42 1/4 x 50 7/8 x 20 1/4 in. [107.3 x 129.2 x 51.4 cm]; overall width 41 7/8 in. [106.4 cm])
Courtesy of the artist

Sarah Cain
***smc shrine*, 2011**
Mixed-media installation on floor and display case walls (near side)
Dimensions variable (approx. 29 1/2 x 28 1/4 x 25 in. [74.9 x 71.8 x 63.5 cm])
Courtesy of the artist

Sarah Cain and George Herms
***Untitled*, 2011**
Installation of titles handwritten in felt-tip pen on paper pattern pieces, located on display case walls (far side)
Dimensions variable
Courtesy of the artist

On floor (*Lemon Bar* table):
George Herms
***Lemon Bar (Untitled Wood Paddle)*, 2011**
Found-object sculpture
Approx. 11 3/8 x 25 x 14 in. (28.9 x 63.5 x 35.6 cm)
Courtesy of the artist

George Herms
***Lemon Bar (Song)*, 2011**
Found-object sculpture
Approx. 11 1/4 x 9 1/4 x 6 1/4 in.
(28.6 x 23.5 x 15.9 cm)
Courtesy of the artist

George Herms
***Lemon Bar (Centerpiece)*, 2011**
Found-object sculpture
Approx. 28 3/4 x 12 1/4 x 15 3/4 in.
(73 x 31.1 x 40 cm)
Courtesy of the artist

George Herms
***Lemon Bar (P.R.)*, 2011**
Found-object sculpture
Approx. 12 7/8 x 7 1/4 x 4 1/2 in.
(32.7 x 18.4 x 11.4 cm)
Courtesy of the artist

George Herms
***Lemon Bar (Beyond H. D.)*, 2011**
Found-object sculpture
Approx. 24 5/8 x 22 x 14 in.
(62.5 x 55.9 x 35.6 cm)
Courtesy of the artist

Ceiling (suspended):
George Herms
***5 BBQ MoonRocks*, 2011**
Five suspended plastic and wire sculptures
(1) Approx. 15 x 17 x 16 3/4 in.
(38.1 x 43.1 x 42.5 cm)
(2) Approx. 13 x 19 x 20 1/4 in.
(33 x 48.3 x 51.3 cm)
(3) Approx. 21 1/2 x 19 1/4 x 18 3/4 in.
(54.6 x 48.9 x 47.6 cm)
(4) Approx. 20 1/2 x 14 1/2 x 18 1/4 in.
(52 x 36.8 x 46.4 cm)
(5) Approx. 27 1/4 x 27 x 15 in.
(69.2 x 68.6 x 38.1 cm)
Courtesy of the artist

Stanya Kahn and Llyn Foulkes

Happy Song for You, 2011
HD video, color, sound
5:07 min.
Courtesy of the artists

Shana Lutker and John Baldessari

A–>B, 2011
Mixed-media installation: 2 tables, assorted objects, 2 flat-screen monitors, 2 digital cameras, existing and constructed walls, and wall vinyl
Dimensions variable (constructed U-shaped outer wall: height 96 1/4 in. [244.5 cm], length of back 181 3/8 in. [460.7 cm], length of arms 60 5/8 in. [154 cm], wall width back and arms 5 1/8 in. [13 cm]; tables: 29 1/4 x 44 x 78 1/4 in. each [74.3 x 111.8 x 198.8 cm]; monitors: 44 in. [111.8 cm] each)
Courtesy of the artists

Amanda Ross-Ho and Allen Ruppersberg

The Meaning of Plus and Minus, 2011
Mixed-media installation: green pedestal, fabricated binder sculpture, random-sequence digital slide show, and moving-image projection with audio (music)
Overall dimensions variable; pedestal: 24 3/4 x 72 x 35 7/8 in. (62.9 x 182.9 x 91.1 cm); binder: 51 3/4 x 45 1/4 x 29 3/4 in. (131.4 x 114.9 x 75.6 cm) (width at spine: 10 in. [25.4 cm]; width at open end of binder: 29 3/4 in. [75.6 cm])
Courtesy of the artists; Cherry and Martin, Los Angeles; Margo Leavin Gallery, Los Angeles; and Mitchell-Innes and Nash, New York

Robert Williams and Ed Moses

Robert Williams
***Swap Meet Sally,* 2005**
Oil on canvas
36 x 30 in. (91.4 x 76.2 cm)
Courtesy of Tony Shafrazi Gallery, New York

Robert Williams
***Gimme, Gimme, Gimme,* 2007**
Oil on canvas
30 x 40 in. (76.2 x 101.6 cm)
Private collection; courtesy of Tony Shafrazi Gallery, New York

Robert Williams
***Wrangling the Firmament*, 2008**
Oil on canvas
36 x 48 in. (91.4 x 121.9 cm)
Courtesy of Tony Shafrazi, New York

Robert Williams
***Creation Trumps Creator*, 2010**
Oil on canvas
36 x 30 in. (91.4 x 76.2 cm)
Collection of Suzanne Williams

Ed Moses
***Dance of the Snake*, 2011**
Acrylic on fabric
72 x 48 in. (182.9 x 121.9 cm)
Courtesy of the artist

Ed Moses
***Hed-Owt #2*, 2011**
Acrylic on fabric
72 x 48 in. (182.9 x 121.9 cm)
Courtesy of the artist

Ed Moses
***Hed-Owt #3*, 2011**
Acrylic on fabric
72 x 48 in. (182.9 x 121.9 cm)
Courtesy of the artist

Ed Moses
***Me*, 2011**
Acrylic on fabric
72 x 48 in. (182.9 x 121.9 cm)
Courtesy of the artist

Reproduction Credits

All artworks are © the artists. Installation photographs are of the exhibition *Two Schools of Cool* unless otherwise noted. Except as noted below, all photographs are by Joshua White, J.W. Pictures, Inc., Los Angeles. Numbers refer to the page on which an image appears.

Photo: Christopher Bliss: p. 59
Courtesy of Stanya Kahn and Llyn Foulkes: pp. 34, 40–43
Courtesy of Amanda Ross-Ho: pp. 60, 68
Courtesy of Allen Ruppersberg: p. 69
Photo: Alan Shaffer; courtesy of Ed Moses studio: p. 84
Photo: Blue Trimarchi: pp. 81, 82; courtesy of the artist and Tony Shafrazi Gallery, New York: p. 80
Photo: Joshua White; courtesy of Honor Fraser Gallery: p. 29

Staff

Kate Andersen
Donor Relations Associate

Sarah C. Bancroft
Curator

Kelly Bishop
Family and Public Programs Manager

Ed Bopp
Assistant Registrar

Ursula Cyga
Office Manager/Museum Services

Adrian De La Pena
Maintenance and Facilities

Doris Dialogu
Visitor Services Associate

Paulette Gibson
Director of Finance

Bridget Jesionowski-McKay
Individual Gifts Officer

Albert Lopez Jr.
Operations Director

Fatima Manalili
Curatorial Associate

Dorothy McClelland
Tour and Studio Programs Assistant

Hayley Miller
Director of Visitor Services

Karen Moss
Adjunct Curator

Glenn Peters
Deputy Director

Johnny Sampson
Curatorial Associate

Anna-Marie Sanchez
Exhibitions and Collections Manager

Jeanette Saunders
Registrar

Kirsten Schmidt
Director of Marketing and Communications

Steve Schmidt
Security Coordinator

Darcy Schwier
Event Manager

Lisa A. Silagyi
Director of Education and Public Programs

Kelly Smith
Senior Accountant

Jenni Stenson
School and Tour Programs Manager

Dennis Szakacs
Director

Fellows of Contemporary Art

Fellows of Contemporary Art Members
As of August 1, 2011

Allison and Paul Alanis
Dewey Anderson
Judith and Alex Angerman
Barbara and Charles Arledge
Leisa and David Austin
Rhona Bader
Franziska and Raoul Balcaen
Katherine Bard
Gail and George Baril
Beatrix and Gardy Barker
Pat Barkley
Ann and Olin Barrett
Geoffrey Beaumont
Nancy Berman and Alan Bloch
Lanie Bernhard
Roberta and Ronald Bloom
Joan Borinstein
Linda Brownridge and Edward Mulvaney
Gay and Ernest Bryant
Bente and Gerald E. Buck
JoAnn and Ron Busuttil
Susan and John Caldwell
Mary and Gus Chabre
Britt and Don Chadwick
Charlotte Chamberlain, PhD, and Paul Wieselmann, PhD
Heidi Chang
Judy and Jin Chang
Ellen and Joe Checota
Susan Cherney
Mary Leigh Cherry and Tony de los Reyes
Jan and Joe Cobert
Barbara Cohn
Lynn and Carl Cooper
Francine and Herb Cooper
Zoe and Don Cosgrove
Beryl Cowley
Marina Forstmann Day and Paul Livadary
Barbara and Marcus de León
Laurie and Jon Deer
Marla Diamond
Linda Dickason
Grace and Richard Dickman
Carole and Robert Edelstein
Eric Egaas and Stephen Rose
Lucille Epstein
Leslie Falick and Norman Koplof
Judy and Kent Frewing
Bonnie Levin Friedman and Robert Friedman
Lisa and Jerry Friedman
Christine From
Joel Gilman
Beverly and Bruce Gladstone
Sirje Helder Gold and Michael Gold
Homeira and Arnold Goldstein
Donna Gottlieb
Beverly Haas
Roberta Haft and Howard Rosoff
Ellen Hageman
Carol Halperin
Nancy Hardin
Marcia Harrow
Jeanne and Fredrick Henry
Linda Hindley
Robin and Edgar Hirst
John Hokom
Essie and David Horwitz
Roberta Baily Huntley
Ellen and Jimmy Isenson
Freya and Mark Ivener
Lisa and Jim Jeffs
Gloria and Sonny Kamm
JoAnn and Charles Kaplan
Joshua Kaplan
Tobe and Greg Karns
Nancy and Bernie Kattler
Nancy and Jonathan Kaye
Isabel and Harvey Kibel
Gina Knox and Richard Mull
Monique Konovalov and David Monzon
Charlene and Sanford Kornblum
Kaaren Kurtzman
Daniel Lara and Carlyn Aguilar
Larry Layne and Sheelagh Boyd
Dawn Hoffman Lee and Harlan Lee
Lydia and Chuck Levy
Raquel and Bertram Lewitt
Penny and Jay Lusche
Linda Maggard
Marilyn Mahan
Barbara Maxwell
Peter Mays and York Chang
Meher McArthur
Hillary Metz
Marcia Metzger
Marla and Jeffrey Michaels
Carolyn and Charles Miller
Peggy Miller
Cindy Miscikowski
Michael Moore
Kay Mortenson and R. Kelly
Wendy Moss
Garna Muller
Ann and Bob Myers
Shulamit Nazarian
Lois and Richard Neiter
Sandra Nichols
Gwen and Peter Norton
Richard Orselli
Cathie and David Partridge
Gordana and Stephen Perlof
Agnes and Phil Peters
Tom Peters
Sheila Poncher
Joel Portnoy
Gina Russ and Irving Posalski
Jeffrey Rapp and Neil Silverman
Joan Rehnborg
Irene and Eytan Ribner
Debby and Bill Richards
Karen and Richard Rosenberg
Lori and Adam Saitman
June Sattler
Kathleen Schaefer and Richard Frank
Carole Schiffer
Lora Schlesinger
Sherie and Alan Schneider
Marcia and Dick Schulman
Wendy and Ron Schwartz
Jennifer and Anton Segerstrom
Zina Sherman
Gilena and Gary Simons
Pam Smith
Ronnie and Joe Stabler
Laurie Smits Staude
Carol and Jay Stein
MC Sungaila
I. H. Sutnick
Jocelyn Tetel
Margot Smith Thomas
Vera Tsai
Sue Tsao
Geoffrey Tuck and David Richards
Elinor and Rubin Turner
Dallas Price-Van Breda and Bob Van Breda
Jessie and Bill Van Lieshout
Carolyn and Bob Volk
Suzette Wachtel
Toby and Bob Waldrof
Janice and Daniel Wallace
Fern Wallace
Kathy Watt
Bob Weekley
Linda and Tod White
Jene M. Witte
Annette and Herb Wolas
Laura-Lee and Robert Woods
Charity Wu
Meeson Pae Yang
Sandee Young

Curator's Award exhibitions initiated and sponsored by the Fellows of Contemporary Art

The concept of the Fellows of Contemporary Art, as developed by its founding members in 1975, is unique. Membership dues are used to initiate and sponsor exhibitions for emerging and midcareer California artists, to publish outstanding professional catalogs and other documents, to encourage a broad range of exhibition sites, and to provide stimulating educational experiences for the members. The intention is to collaborate with the art community at large and to nurture the expression of creative freedom.

2011
Two Schools of Cool
Sarah C. Bancroft, curator
Orange County Museum of Art, Newport Beach, California
October 9, 2011–January 22, 2012

2009
Superficiality and Superexcrescence: Surface and Identity in Recent California Art
Chris Bedford, Kristina Newhouse, and Jennifer Wulffson, curators
Ben Maltz Gallery, Otis College of Art and Design, Los Angeles
June 27–September 12

2007
Kori Newkirk: 1997–2007
Thelma Golden, curator
The Studio Museum in Harlem, New York
November 14, 2007–March 16, 2008

2005
Thing: New Sculpture from Los Angeles
James Elaine, Aimee Chang, and Christopher Miles, curators
Hammer Museum, Los Angeles
February 6–June 5

2004
Topographies
Karen Moss, curator
San Francisco Art Institute
March 19–May 8

2003
George Stone: Probabilities—A Mid-career Survey
Carole Ann Klonarides, curator
Los Angeles Municipal Art Gallery
September 9–November 16

Whiteness, A Wayward Construction
Tyler Stallings, curator
Laguna Art Museum, Laguna Beach, California
March 16–July 6

2002
On Wanting to Grow Horns: The Little Theater of Tom Knechtel
Anne Ayers, curator
Ben Maltz Gallery, Otis College of Art and Design, Los Angeles
November 9, 2002–February 15, 2003

Michael Brewster: See Hear Now—A Sonic Drawing and Five Acoustic Sculptures
Irene Tsatsos, curator
Los Angeles Contemporary Exhibitions
February 16–April 20

2000
Flight Patterns
Connie Butler, curator
The Museum of Contemporary Art, Los Angeles
November 12, 2000–February 11, 2001

1999
Bruce and Norman Yonemoto: Memory, Matter, and Modern Romance
Karin Higa, curator
Japanese American National Museum, Los Angeles
January 23–July 4

Eleanor Antin
Howard N. Fox, curator
Los Angeles County Museum of Art
May 23–August 23

1998
Access All Areas
Japanese American Cultural and Community Center, Los Angeles
June 6–July 26

1997
Scene of the Crime
Ralph Rugoff, curator
UCLA at the Armand Hammer Museum of Art and Cultural Center, Los Angeles
July 22–October 5

1995
Llyn Foulkes: Between a Rock and a Hard Place
Marilu Knode, curator
Laguna Art Museum, Laguna Beach, California
October 27, 1995–January 21, 1996

1994
Plane/Structures
David Pagel, curator
Otis Gallery, Otis College of Art and Design, Los Angeles
September 10–November 5

1993
Kim Abeles: Encyclopedia Persona, A Fifteen-Year Survey
Karen Moss, curator
Santa Monica Museum of Art, Santa Monica, California
September 23–December 6

1992
Proof: Los Angeles Art and the Photograph, 1960–1980
Charles Desmarais, curator
Laguna Art Museum, Laguna Beach, California
October 31, 1992–January 17, 1993

1991
Facing the Finish: Some Recent California Art
Robert Riley and John Caldwell, curators
San Francisco Museum of Modern Art
September 20–December 1

Roland Reiss: A Seventeen-Year Survey
Betty Ann Brown, curator
Los Angeles Municipal Art Gallery
November 19, 1991–January 19, 1992

1990
Lita Albuquerque: Reflections
Henry Hopkins, curator
Santa Monica Museum of Art, Santa Monica, California
January 19–April 1

1989
The Pasadena Armory Show 1989
Noel Korten, curator
The Armory Center for the Arts, Pasadena, California
November 2, 1989–January 31, 1990

1988
Jud Fine
Ronald Onorato, curator
La Jolla Museum of Contemporary Art, La Jolla, California
August 19–October 2

1987
Variations III: Emerging Artists in Southern California
Melinda Wortz, curator
Los Angeles Contemporary Exhibitions
April 22–May 31

Perpetual Motion
Betty Turnbull, curator
Santa Barbara Museum of Art, Santa Barbara, California
November 17, 1987–January 24, 1988

1986
William Brice
Ann Goldstein, curator
The Museum of Contemporary Art, Los Angeles
September 1–October 19

1985
Sunshine and Shadow: Recent Painting in Southern California
Dr. Susan Larsen, curator
Fisher Gallery, University of Southern California, Los Angeles
January 15–February 23

James Turrell
Julia Brown, curator
The Museum of Contemporary Art, Los Angeles
November 13, 1985–February 9, 1986

1984
Martha Alf Retrospective
Josine Ianco-Starrels, curator
Los Angeles Municipal Art Gallery
March 6–April 1

1983
Variations II: Seven Los Angeles Painters
Constance Mallinson, curator
Gallery at the Plaza, Security Pacific National Bank, Los Angeles
May 8–June 30

1982
Changing Trends: Content and Style–Twelve Southern California Painters
Robert Smith, curator
Laguna Beach Museum of Art, Laguna Beach, California
November 18, 1982–January 3, 1983

1981
Craig Kauffman: Comprehensive Survey, 1957–1980
Robert McDonald, curator
La Jolla Museum of Contemporary Art, La Jolla, California
March 14–May 3

Paul Wonner: Abstract Realist
George Neubert, curator
San Francisco Museum of Modern Art
October 1–November 22

1980
Variations: Five Los Angeles Painters
Bruce Hiles and Donald Brewer, curators
University Art Galleries, University of Southern California, Los Angeles
October 20–November 23

1979
Vija Celmins: A Survey Exhibition
Betty Turnbull, curator
Newport Harbor Art Museum, Newport Beach, California
December 15, 1979–February 3, 1980

1978
Wallace Berman Retrospective
Hal Glicksman, curator
Otis Gallery, Otis Art Institute, Los Angeles
October 24–November 25

1977
Unstretched Surfaces / Surfaces Libres
Jean-Luc Bordeaux, Jean-Francois de Canchy, and Alfred Pacquement, curators
Los Angeles Institute of Contemporary Art
November 5–December 16

1976
Ed Moses: Drawings, 1958–1976
Joseph Masheck, curator
Frederick S. Wight Art Gallery, University of California, Los Angeles
July 13–August 15

Contributors

Sarah C. Bancroft joined the Orange County Museum of Art as curator in May 2008. In addition to organizing *Two Schools of Cool*, Bancroft curated the traveling exhibition *Richard Diebenkorn: The Ocean Park Series* (2011–12) and the 2010 California Biennial. In 2009 she curated *Video Work by Gao Shiquang and Chen Qiulin* at OCMA as part of the Ancient Paths, Modern Voices China Festival, organized by Carnegie Hall and the Segerstrom Center for the Arts, and she coordinated OCMA's presentation of the exhibition *Carlos Amorales: Discarded Spider*. Bancroft previously worked at the Solomon R. Guggenheim Museum in New York, where she cocurated *James Rosenquist: A Retrospective* (2003) with the late, great Walter Hopps and coordinated a masterpiece exhibition from the permanent collection that traveled to Rome and Tokyo. She received her MA in the history of art from the Courtauld Institute of Art in London in 2000. Just prior to moving to Orange County, she spent six months traveling from Stockholm to Rome conducting PhD research pertaining to the tour of James Rosenquist's monumental painting *F-111* through Europe in the mid-1960s. Her area of specialization is American art from the 1950s to the present.

Constance Lewallen is adjunct curator at the University of California Berkeley Art Museum and Pacific Film Archive. As senior curator at the museum from 1998 to June 2007, she curated many major exhibitions, including *Joe Brainard: A Retrospective* (2001); *Dream of the Audience: Theresa Hak Kyung Cha (1951–1982)* (2001); *Everything Matters: Paul Kos, a Retrospective* (2003); *Ant Farm (1968–1978)* (2004); and *A Rose Has No Teeth: Bruce Nauman in the 1960s* (2007). All these exhibitions toured nationally or internationally and were accompanied by catalogs. Her exhibition *Allen Ruppersberg: You and Me or the Art of Give and Take* was presented at the Santa Monica Museum of Art in fall 2009. Lewallen was cocurator with Karen Moss of *State of Mind: New California Art ca. 1970*, which opened at the Orange County Museum of Art in October 2011.

Phyllis Lutjeans is the former curator of education and performance art at the Newport Harbor Art Museum (precursor of the Orange County Museum of Art), where she worked from 1968 to 1982. She was an unwitting collaborator in the artist Chris Burden's performance *TV Hijack* (1972), in which Burden took Lutjeans hostage during a live broadcast of the public access art program that she hosted. Lutjeans cofounded TLK Gallery with Betty Turnbull and Victoria Kogan in Costa Mesa, California (gallery active 1982–85), and was a museum scientist and adjunct lecturer at the University of California, Irvine, from 1985 to 1992. In 1992 she founded the Art Crowd salon and has hosted guest speakers in her Irvine living room for nearly twenty years. The Art Crowd engages in intimate dialogue concerning contemporary art issues with national and international artists, museum curators, art critics, gallery owners, collectors, art historians, and others. Lutjeans continues to give lectures and write essays for exhibition catalogs. She is currently writing a book on contemporary art and experience.

Andy Moses is an artist who lives and works in Venice, California. He was born in Los Angeles in 1962 and attended California Institute of the Arts from 1979 to 1982. At CalArts he focused on performance, film, and painting, studying with Michael Asher, John Baldessari, and Douglas Huebler. In 1982 he moved to New York, where he developed a kind of process-driven painting that is simultaneously abstract and representational. He is interested in pushing the physical properties of paint through chemical reactions, viscosity interference, and gravity to create elaborate compositions that mimic nature and its forces. He had his first solo show in New York at Annina Nosei Gallery in 1987 and has continued to exhibit his work in New York, Los Angeles, and abroad over the past twenty-five years. He moved back to Los Angeles in 2000.

Catherine Taft is a writer and curator based in Los Angeles. She is a regular contributor to journals such as *Artforum*, *Metropolis M*, *Art Review*, and *Modern Painters* and to exhibition catalogs in the United States and abroad. In addition to her writing, Taft is curatorial associate and project specialist in the Department of Architecture and Contemporary Art at the Getty Research Institute, where she helped organize the exhibitions *California Video* (2008) and *Pacific Standard Time: Crosscurrents in L.A. Painting and Sculpture, 1950–1970* (2011).